CADRES OF TIBET

Also by Jayadeva Ranade

Rs. 1095.00 | 9789381904435 | Hardback

Forthcoming title by author

Xi Jinping's China

Rs. 1400.00 | 9789386288905 | Hardback

CADRES OF TIBET

JAYADEVA RANADE

KNOWLEDGE WORLD

KW Publishers Pvt Ltd
New Delhi

ISBN 978-93-86288-92-9 Hardback
ISBN 978-93-86288-93-6 ebook

Published in India by Kalpana Shukla

KNOWLEDGE WORLD

KW Publishers Pvt Ltd
4676/21, First Floor, Ansari Road
Daryaganj, New Delhi 110002
Phone: +91 11 23263498/43528107
Marketing: knowledgeworld@kwpub.com
Editorial: jose@kwpub.com
Website: www.kwpub.com

Printed and Bound in India.

Contents

PREFACE

Persons studying matters relating to Tibet, as I have for about four decades now, realise that while there is a lot of data on the Tibet Autonomous Region (TAR) available in China's official media, but before information concerning the cadres who govern the Tibet Autonomous Region (TAR) is very scanty and not available in one place. Similarly, information on some key aspects of China's policies on Tibet is not available in one place. When available, the information is piecemeal and scattered and, therefore, denied to most.

This book is an initial attempt to make pertinent information on Tibet readily available to an interested reader. Constraints of time and resources restricted my efforts to include more information. For the same reason it was not possible to include in this book details of those officers of the People's Liberation Army (PLA) with Tibet experience and who would have a voice in Tibet affairs.

The emphasis is on presenting brief biographical sketches of the relatively more important cadres to enable the analyst and reader to form an impression about the individual, his future career prospects and possibly his affiliations. Readers will notice the additional focus on cadres of the Tibet Central Administration in Lhasa and those of the Lhasa Municipality. The book identifies, in most cases, the ethnicity of the cadres. These cadres are largely expected to stay involved in Tibet affairs for the next decade and some of them can be identified as possible successors to the current TAR Party Secretary Wu Yingjie.

The book briefly discusses the Aid Tibet Programme. The programme's importance lies in the fact that it has ensured the exposure of many CCP cadres across China to the conditions in Tibet and had an important influence on their career paths. Consequently, over the years it has built a cohort of CCP cadres with a stake in the CCP and the central government's policies on Tibet.

In this context, the bio-sketches of the previous surviving TAR Party Secretaries would also be useful along with the list of CCP cadres who continue to wield influence in decisions on Tibet. Many are today in the Politburo.

Much of the information in this book on the TAR's Administrative Districts and governmental and Party structure is from the official Chinese media. Most of the other information, especially the biographical sketches, are on the basis of inputs from various reliable sources who regrettably can not be named.

The Tibet Policy Institute (TPI) generously made available their compilation of TAR officials which is in Tibetan. Ms Apa Lhamo, a Research Associate at the Centre for China Analysis and Strategy (CCAS) was of invaluable assistance in the compilation, translation, and in cross-checking inputs for the book.

Abbreviations

CCP	Communist Party of China
CPPCC	Chinese People's Political Consultative Conference Committee
TAR	Tibet Autonomous Region
CC	Central Committee
CDIC	Central Discipline Inspection Commission
UFWD	United Front Work Department

Source: Googlemaps

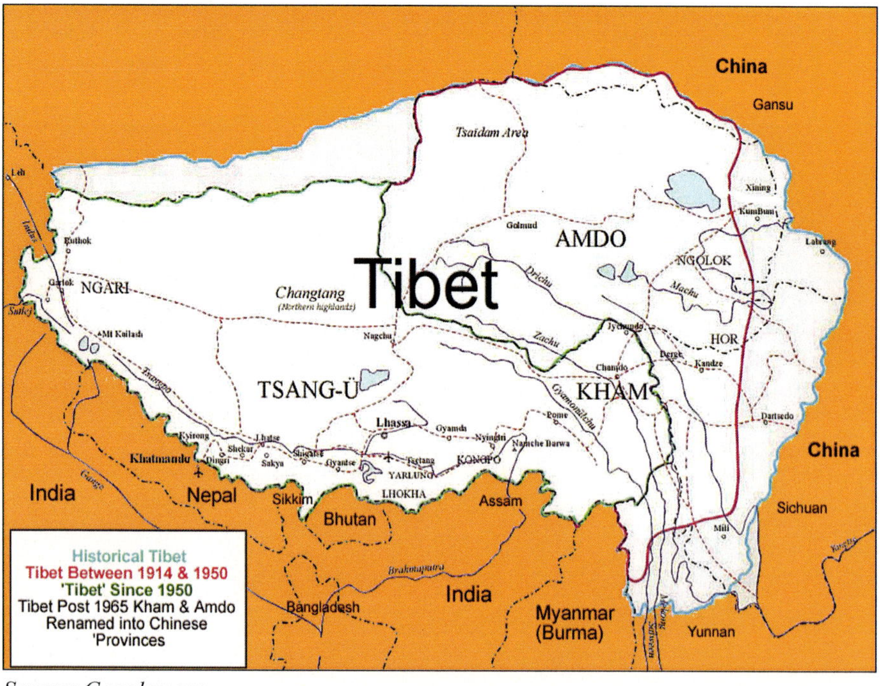

Source: Googlemaps

Information shown on these drawings/maps/charts is compiled from numerous sources and may not be complete or accurate.

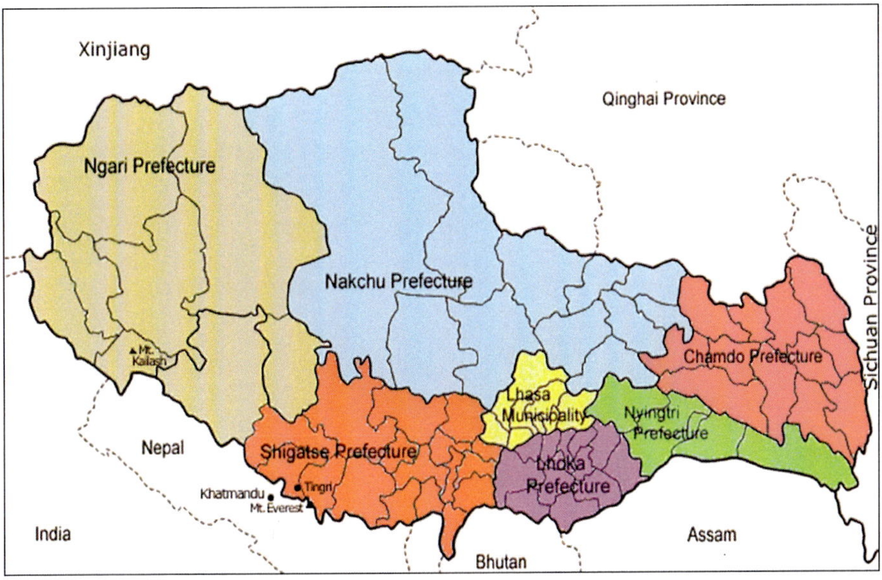

Source: Googlemaps (Administrative Divisions of Tibet by CCP)

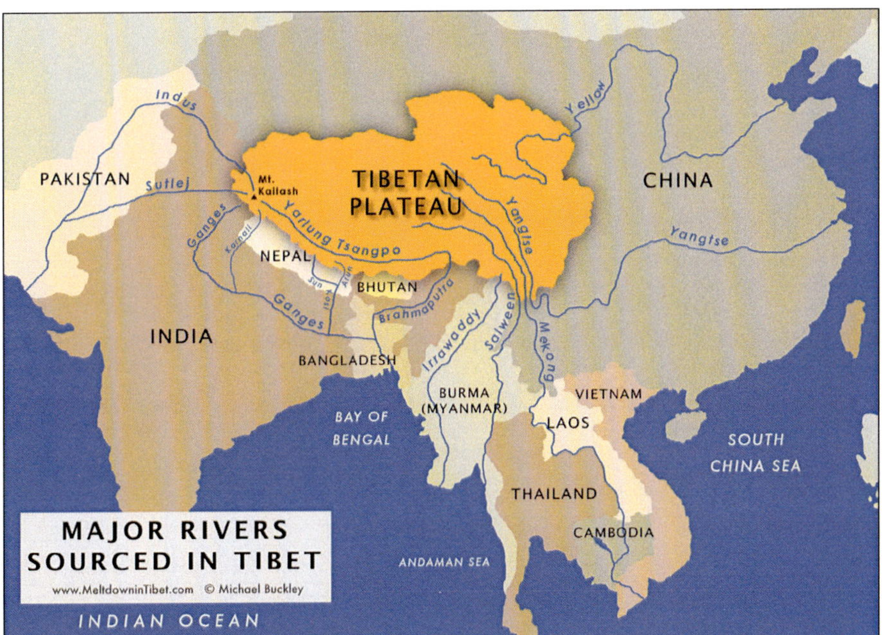

Source: www.meltdowninTibet.com

Information shown on these drawings/maps/charts is compiled from numerous sources and may not be complete or accurate.

Tibetan Autonomous Region (TAR)

Following the 'liberation' of Tibet by the People's Republic of China (PRC)'s People's Liberation Army (PLA) on May 23, 1951, the central communist authorities in Beijing truncated the erstwhile Tibet and created the Tibet Autonomous Region (TAR) on September 01, 1965. Parts of the old Tibet were incorporated into the Qinghai, Gansu, and Sichuan provinces though they were allowed to retain their minority characteristics and designated autonomous prefectures. The TAR now covers approx. 1.2 million sq. kms. or one eighth of China's total land area (Tibet formerly covered 2.5 million sq. km). Map of Greater Tibet is at Appendix.

TAR borders Myanmar, India, Bhutan and Nepal in the south, India in the west, the Xinjiang-Uighur Autonomous Region and Qinghai province of China in the north, and Yunnan province of China in the east. It has terrain descending northwest to southeast, with the average elevation decreasing from over 5,000 metres to 4,000 meters.

TAR has over 20 rivers, each with a drainage area of over 10,000 sq. km. Some of the rivers in Tibet flow into the sea while the others are just inland waters. Most of the rivers that ultimately empty into the Pacific Ocean or the Indian Ocean are distributed in the border areas of east, south and west Tibet. They include the Jinshajiang River (the upper reaches of the Yangtze River), Dza Chu (Mekong), and Gyalmo Nyulchu (Salween) in the east; the Yarlung Tsangpo (Brahmaputra) in the south; and Langchen Khabab (Xiangquan River) and Sengge Khabab (also called Shiquan River in the upper reaches of the Indus) in the west. Many of Tibet's rivers have potential for hydroelectric development.

There are more than 1000 lakes in TAR, which cover a total area of 23,800 sq.kms. Namtso (Mongolian: Namco) is the largest lake.

The potential of mineral resources in TAR is estimated at Yuan 650 billion (US$ 86 billion). More than 100 kinds of minerals have been discovered in Tibet, of which 36 have proven reserves and rank among the top five deposits in China.

Years ago, the PRC Geological Survey Team discovered five ferrous and non-ferrous metal deposits along the route of the Qinghai-Tibet Railway with total reserves of one billion tonnes of iron ore, 30 million tonnes of copper and 40 million tonnes of lead and zinc.

Tibet is rich in hydro, geothermal, solar and wind energy. It has the potential to produce approximately 200 million kilowatts of natural hydro-electricity annually, about 30 percent of China's total resources in this area. It has 354.8 billion cubic metres of surface water resources, 13.5 percent of the total, and 330 billion cubic metres of glacial water resources. TAR has more than 1,000 sites with prospective geothermal energy reserves. Its geothermal heat discharge is 550,000 kilocalories per second. The Yangbajian Geothermal field in Damxung is currently China's largest high-temperature geothermal field. The water temperature ranges around 93-172°C. Tibet is the leader in China in geothermal energy.

Bon is the oldest religion of Tibet and has 88 monasteries and more than 3,000 resident monks. Buddhism is the main religion of Tibet with four main sects namely Gelugpa, Kargyupa, Sakyapa, and Nyingmapa. At present there are 1,787 monasteries and nunneries of Tibetan Buddhism in the region, with 46,000 resident monks and nuns. In addition there is one church and 700 Christians and 4 mosques and 2,000 Muslims in TAR.

The total length of highways in TAR is 43,717 km with all radiating out of Lhasa; of these there are 15 main highways and 315 subsidiary highways. The most important among them are the Qinghai-Tibet Highway, Sichuan-Tibet Highway, Xinjiang-Tibet Highway, Yunnan-Tibet Highway and the Nepal-Tibet Highway.

Construction of the 1,142 km section of the Qinghai -Tibet Railway from Golmud to Lhasa formally started On June 29, 2001 and was completed on October 12, 2005 at a cost of US$ 3.68 billion. It was opened to regular passenger traffic on July 1, 2006. More than 960 km of the Qinghai-Tibet railway is at an altitude of above 4,000 metres. It has 675 bridges.

China has confirmed plans to extend the railway in Tibet to the borders with India, Bhutan and Nepal by 2020, and it plans to construct a new line east from Lhasa close to India's border, in a new strategic network. The Chinese state media announced the beginning of construction of a new line to Nyingtri in 2014, just opposite the Indian state of Arunachal Pradesh, which China claims as part of the PRC. The new rail links follow the opening of a new checkpoint and 'land port' on Tibet's border with Nepal in October (2014) and preceded the opening of the Nathula pass route from Sikkim in India to the sacred Mount Kailash in Tibet, which was announced in September 2014. The planned new construction follows completion of the first phase of extension of the Qinghai-Lhasa railway to Shigatse in TAR, which was inaugurated in August 2014. Work is now in progress to extend this line to Nyingtri Prefecture in the southeast of the Tibet Autonomous Region (TAR).

China plans to link western Tibet's Ngari Prefecture by rail from neighbouring Xinjiang (East Turkestan) and Tibet's Shigatse prefecture, and to start building the Sichuan-Tibet railway in 2016. China's online Tibet news service said on March 14, 2015 that a proposal for this was presented during the "Two Sessions" in early March by Losang Sherdun, a CPPCC (Chinese People's Political Consultative Conference) member from Ngari. Losang Sherdun, a member of the CPPCC's National Committee and Vice Chairman of the regional PPCC of Ngari Prefecture, had called for further extension of the Southern Xinjiang Railway and Lhasa-Shigatse Railway to Ngari.

The railway and its connection to Shigatse has been crucial in the expansion of mining in Tibet, making it possible to transport more ores out of Tibetan areas, many of which were previously remote and inaccessible. The new railway lines are among several new planned routes that will either traverse or terminate on the Tibetan plateau. They represent a dramatic increase in the number and capacity of linkages with the rest of Mainland China's rail network and will facilitate large-scale exploitation of Tibet's natural resources as well as movement of civil, military and cargo traffic into Tibet.

The routes under discussion include two railway lines through some of the most culturally significant as well as restive areas of Tibet. The ambitious plans were finalised by China's Minister of Railways Liu Zhijun, presently serving a suspended death sentence, commuted to life in prison, for corruption. The expansion of communications infrastructure in Tibet is likely to have a major adverse impact on Tibet's environment and landscape. Just weeks after the opening of the Qinghai-Tibet railway in 2006, the Chinese state media announced that fissures had begun to develop in its concrete structures due to the sinking and cracking of its permafrost foundation. China's climate scientists have now warned that warming temperatures, together with the boom in infrastructure construction and urbanization, are combining to create irreversible damage in the ecosystem, including the predicted disappearance of large areas of grasslands, alpine meadows, wetlands and permafrost on the Tibetan plateau by 2050.

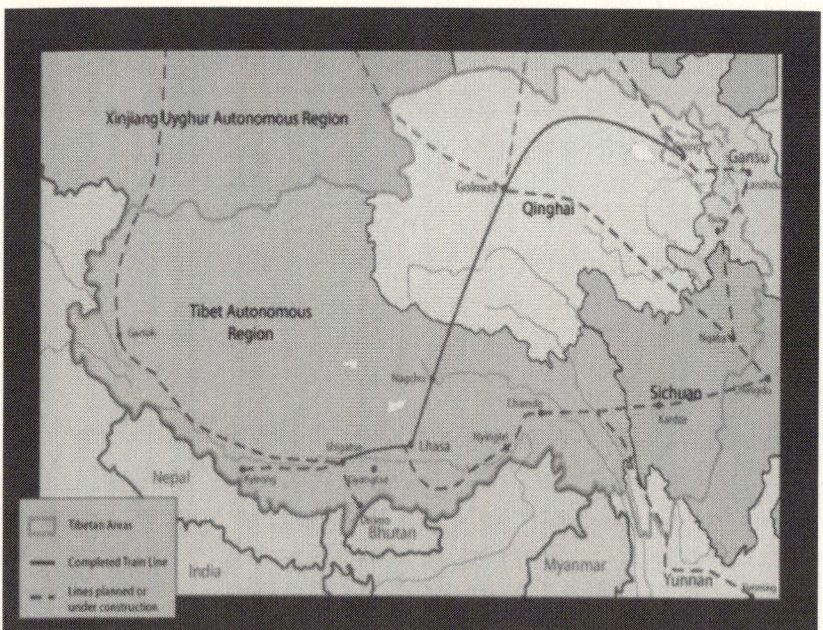

Map: Courtesy-savetibet.org

China's official China Daily had reported on March 14, 2015, that the Sichuan delegation at the annual session of the National People's Congress, China's version of a parliament, had called for incorporation of the construction of the Sichuan-Tibet railway in the country's next five-year plan to commence in 2016. The planned 1,800-km line will connect Chengdu, capital of Sichuan province, with Lhasa, capital of Tibet, and construction will cost 200 billion Yuan (US$ 32 billion). The report additionally noted that the Chinese government has approved the construction of sections linking Lhasa to Nyingchi in eastern TAR, and Chengdu to Ya'an in western Sichuan.

China's official Xinhua news agency confirmed in March 2016, that the "Sichuan-Tibet Railway" had been listed in the draft outline of the 13th Five-Year Plan (2016-2020) released on March 5, 2016. Subsequently, following interviews with Chengdu's Development and Reform Committee, another Chinese state-run media "People's Web" reported that the Sichuan-Tibet railway would be one of the five new railways connecting Chengdu with the capitals of neighbouring provinces.

Details available from Chinese state-run media list the proposed stations along the new railway line as: Dartsedo City (Ch: Kangding), Yaknga City (Ch:Ya'an), Chamdo City (Ch: Changdu), and Nyingchi City (Ch: Linzhi), making four separate sections: Chengdu to Yaknga; Yaknga to Darzedo; Dartsedo to Nyingchi; and Nyingchi to Lhasa.

The estimated travel time between Chengdu and Lhasa will be 15 hours, compared to the present 42 hours via the Qinghai-Tibet railway. There is, however, some discrepancy in the length of the railway. The China Daily and Xinhua state that the length of the new Chengdu-Tibet railway will be about 1,629 km, while the People's Web mentions the operating length as around 1,900 km and construction length as approximately 1,800 km.

Construction of the Chengdu to Yaknga section has already begun and will be completed in 2018. China's National Development and Reform Commission had already earlier approved the Chengdu to Dartsedo section. Construction of the Lyingchi to Lhasa section was started in December 2014.

Discussing the difficulties in construction of this railway line, Lin Shijin, a senior civil engineer at China Railway Corporation, told China Daily that

'The accumulated height it will climb reaches more than 14,000 meters, and it will cross many fault zones...It's like the largest roller-coaster in the world. With a designed service life of 100 years, it is believed to be one of the most difficult railway projects to build on Earth.'

Assessments of the impact of this railway on the environment as well as the potential destruction of the vulnerable natural environment at the high plateau are not yet available.

The Aid Tibet Programme

The Aid Tibet program has been underway for over 20 years and is now well established. It was officially launched at the Third Work Conference on Tibet held in 1994 by the Chinese Communist Party (CCP)'s Central Committee (CC). In its present form middle ranking cadres from inland China provinces, the Central ministries in Beijing and large state enterprises sign a 3-year contract to work in Tibet. More than a thousand (1,199 in the 7th wave) arrive in Tibet every three years with hundreds more arriving yearly on shorter ad hoc assignments. Each TAR municipality and prefecture has at least two inland China provinces/ municipalities providing assistance in the form of major infrastructure projects and 'governance enhancement'. The Aid Tibet cadres are then assigned senior political positions largely at the municipality, prefecture and county levels but also occasionally in the TAR-level Party and Government departments. Wu Yingjie, who was appointed TAR's new Party Secretary on August 28, 2016, is an Aid Tibet cadre.

The assisting provinces and Central ministries are expected to pay for the projects they sponsor and in some cases the salaries of the cadres they send to Tibet to implement the projects. It is, in essence, a form of taxation and the amounts of money are huge often totalling anywhere from RMB¥ 300 to 500 million. The assisting provinces and Central ministries like to keep a close eye on how their funds are being spent and therefore demand that their Aid Tibet cadres are assigned key positions from which they can supervise their projects. They want someone they can trust when they call for a project update. In the municipalities and prefectures, the senior Aid Tibet cadres are generally slotted as Deputy Party Secretaries and Deputy Government Administrators. In the counties of the TAR they more often become the Party Secretary to the extent that today most county Party Secretaries are Aid Tibet cadres.

From the TAR Party and Government's point of view, it wants and demands that the inland provinces/cities and Central ministries select and send strong, competent and knowledgeable cadres. There are also inbuilt incentives for the Aid Tibet cadres. Back home their careers usually face stiff competition and sometimes are stalled as a result. In Tibet, usually their new assignments represent a slight promotion with much more responsibility. While they assist with the TAR's "leap frog" economic development, the hope exists that their own careers will take "leap frog" advancement when – and if – they return home! For example, Beijing assists the Lhasa Municipality: Beijing's Party Secretary is Politburo member Guo Jinlong who was Party Secretary in the TAR (2000-2004). One can be sure that he takes a personal interest in Beijing's TAR projects and the cadres from Beijing who are on assignment there. The prospect of accelerated promotion can be a powerful incentive for an ambitious middle level cadre in Beijing to volunteer in Tibet.

The 'Aid Tibet' programme is today spread across the entire Tibet Autonomous Region (TAR) and involves each of China's 25 provinces, 5 Autonomous Regions, 4 Municipalities and 2 Special Administrative Regions and virtually all central-level Party and Government organs. Many prominent universities and State-owned Enterprises (SoEs) also have some involvement. They have established relationships with individual districts, counties and cities in TAR, pledged funds from their budgets, and have seconded valuable personnel to TAR. These linkages are maintained over 3-year cycles. The programme is presently in its 8th 3-year cycle. By virtue of their investments, all provinces and major cities of China now have a solid, well-articulated vested interest in Tibet. For many of the middle ranking cadres who have worked in the TAR in 'Aid Tibet' programmes on loan, their experiences would in most cases have been among the most interesting of their professional lives. Many have by now risen to senior positions in the provinces of China and in ministries in Beijing. They have invested time, blood and money over a quarter of a century and know TAR intimately. Together with their provinces and their cities they now constitute a substantial additional internal Chinese political force that cannot be ignored by any Chinese leader. They will closely scrutinize any policy on Tibet and have a voice in its shaping.

Premier Zhu Rongji and CCP CC General Secretary Jiang Zemin pioneered the 'Develop the West' policies which continued during Hu Jintao's tenure. It created its own bureaucracy. This 'Develop the West' policy complemented and reinforced the 'Aid Tibet' program. The large State-owned Enterprises (SoEs) that wield considerable influence in Beijing were quick to support the 'Develop the West' policy. They too have emerged as additional bulwarks against bold change that might be tempted to push aside policies based on wei-hu wen-ding (维护稳定 or wei-wen for short), i.e. the safe-guarding of stability. The SoEs involved in the energy and mining sectors are very active on the Tibetan Plateau and recruit officials retiring from TAR as advisors and government relations specialists. This category of enterprises and officials adds to the layers of well informed, organized and powerful stake-holders who maintain a vigilant watch over Tibet.

For any General Secretary of the CCP CC in Beijing, therefore, to effect any change of policy regarding Tibet is no longer a matter of just having to persuade the PLA. While the PLA's views on policies regarding Tibet cannot be ignored, the CCP CC General Secretary also has to convince and gain the support of these multiple layers of well informed, organized and potentially powerful stake holders.

CCP Cadres in Tibet (TAR)

As of January 2014, there were 225,200 Chinese Communist Party (CCP) members in the Tibet Autonomous Region (TAR). While specific data on the number of ethnic Tibetan Party members is not available, various accounts estimate the number of non-Han minority nationality Party members at slightly over 185,800. If the Tibetan CCP memberships in Qinghai, Gansu, Sichuan and Yunnan are included then the number might easily surpass 220,000 or more Tibetan nationality Party members. As of 2013, work teams on long term appointment (at least for 5 years) have been based in every one of the 5,453 villages of the TAR. Part of their remit is grass roots recruitment to the Party and Youth League, so the TAR Party membership figures will expand considerably in the not too distant future.

The conservative guess-estimate of 220,000 CCP members, however, eclipses the total population of Tibetans in exile in the world. Even conceding that maybe only 10% actually believe the Party propaganda that is part of their required study, the rest must have at least a minimum loyalty to the Party. Neverthelesss all obtained their jobs and perks compliments of the Party, almost all of them are able to communicate in at least basic Chinese, and all would have a stake in the existing political and economic systems which are completely integrated with China and immune to radical changes in direction over the short-to-middle term. If, therefore, China was to change its policy on Tibet to the extent that a deal could be worked out with the Dalai Lama, and where Tibetans in exile – particularly the younger generations born in exile – felt emboldened to risk a return, these Chinese-speaking Tibetan CCP members no doubt would become targets of the exiles. The native Tibetan Party members, therefore, are going to be extremely wary of proposals for changes in policy that carry the danger of bringing back what they believe may be a tsunami of exiled Tibetans coming for employment. Tibetans in China may harbour the desire to see the Dalai Lama return, but probably not the 2-3 generations of Tibetans born and raised in exile.

Interesting, in this context, is a remark made by the current TAR Party Secretary Wu Yingjie to US diplomats in October 2009, when he claimed that in TAR, 70 percent of the civil servants are ethnic minorities and only 30 percent are ethnic Han.

Party Secretaries of the Tibet Autonomous Region (TAR) (1950-2016)

Zhang Guohua	January 1950 - June 1951 (PLA background)
Fan Ming	June 1951 - December 1951 (PLA background)
Zhang Jingwu	March 1952 - August 1965 (PLA background)
Zhang Guohua	September 1965 - till Cultural Revolution
Ren Rong	August 1971 - March 1980 (PLA background)
Yin Fatang	March 1980 - June 1985 (PLA background)
Wu Jinghua	June 1985 - December 1988
Hu Jintao	December 1988 - November 1992 (later China's President)
Chen Kuiyuan	November 1992 - September 2000
Guo Jinlong	September 2000 - December 2004 (today Politburo member)
Yang Chuantang	December 2004 - November 2005 (today Transport Minister)
Zhang Qingli	November 2005 - August 2011
Chen Quanguo	August 2011 - August 2106 (now Xinjiang Party Secretary)

Brief Biographies of Past Eight and Current Party Secretaries of the TAR

Yin Fatang (December 1980 – November 1985): 90-year old Lt. General Yin Fatang is still active and an energetic spokesman for Tibet. He was a member of the 18th Army that fought the battle of Chamdo in 1950 and arrived in Lhasa in 1951. Much of his career was spent in military and civilian roles in Tibet. Even today he is acknowledged as one of the very few senior Chinese officials who became truly fluent in Tibetan. Yin Fatang personifies the "Spirit of Old Tibet," a propaganda slogan heard often today referring nostalgically to the hard work, dedication and idealism of those Chinese who went to Tibet in the early years.

Even as a 90-year old, Yin Fatang is reported to travel to Tibet once or twice a year. He created the 'Tibet Education Foundation' which he continues to head. This foundation is richly endowed by funds that Yin Fatang managed to get out of China's giant State-owned Enterprises (SoEs) that are operating in Tibet or wish to operate there. He uses the money to build schools and provide scholarships to young Tibetans. He also regularly visits and provides support funding for schools in inland China that host Tibetan students.

Prior to being selected as TAR Party Secretary in 1980, Yin Fatang was close to Deng Xiaoping and Hu Yaobang. Thereafter Yin Fatang successfully managed to maintain close personal relations with Jiang Zemin and Hu Jintao, sharing his insights on the politics, economics and culture of Tibet. Reliable reports state that Yin Fatang is invited to attend every meeting on Tibet held in Beijing as a member or an observer out of respect for his experience and knowledge. As long as he is alive Yin Fatang will be a factor – usually a cautious and conservative factor – in the formulation of Tibet policies. His status is reported to have remained unchanged under Xi Jinping.

Wu Jinghua (November 1985 – November 1988): He died in October 2007. Wu Jinghua is probably the only Party Secretary remembered somewhat fondly by the Tibetan people. Wu Jinghua was a non-Han of the Yi nationality from Yunnan and a longtime protégé of Hu Yaobang.

Hu Jintao (December 1988 – November 1992): born in December 1942 in Henan, Hu Jintao joined the CCP in 1964. Hu Jintao was not too pleased at being appointed TAR Party Secretary at the age of 45, but the post gave him exposure to the PLA and within weeks brought him to the attention of Deng Xiaoping. Hu Jintao was the first civilian to hold the leadership post in Tibet and was surrounded by experienced veterans of the PLA who had their own ideas on how to handle the Tibetans. Hu Jintao proved to a solid Party apparatchik who could be trusted to rigorously implement Party policies in the restive region.

The day after his appointment was announced on December 9, 1988, a large demonstration rocked Lhasa. The People's Armed Police opened fire on the demonstrators killing several Tibetans and seriously wounding a Dutch photographer. Hu Jintao arrived in Lhasa in mid-January 1989. On January 23, Hu Jintao traveled to Shigatse, the seat of the Panchen Lama, where the Panchen Lama delivered a scathing report on China's administration of Tibet, declaring that Chinese rule had resulted in more harm than benefit to Tibetans. He died a few days later, leading many Tibetans to believe that Hu Jintao had a hand in the death of the Panchen Lama.

In early March 1989, massive demonstrations occurred in Lhasa and on April 20, 1989, Hu Jintao referred to the demonstrations as a "major event" in the course of China's 40-year occupation of Tibet. Receiving no clear instructions from Party General Secretary Zhao Ziyang on the use of force, Hu Jintao took the initiative to unilaterally deploy 2,000 People's Liberation Army troops and imposed martial law in Lhasa. Deng Xiaoping was impressed that the TAR Party Secretary had shown initiative and earmarked him for further promotions.

Recognition of Hu Jintao's successful tenure in Tibet came in the summer of 1990 when CCP CC General Secretary Jiang Zemin paid a visit to demonstrate his confidence. Soon after, Hu Jintao was appointed First Secretary of the Tibet Military District CCP Committee. In October 1990, less than 2 years after his posting in Tibet began, Hu Jintao suffered a heart attack and moved back to Beijing. For the next two years, Hu Jintao continued to hold the position of TAR Party Secretary and governed directly from Beijing. In October 1992, Hu Jintao was promoted to the CCP CC Politburo Standing Committee making him the seventh most powerful man in China. In January 1992, Chen Kuiyuan was appointed Deputy Secretary of the Party in Tibet, a move that readied him to take over from Hu Jintao later that year.

After taking over as Party General Secretary Hu Jintao retained a firm grip on Tibet affairs and introduced a more proactive policy to deal with foreign governments who officially received the Dalai Lama. China began penalising them with unofficial suspension of trade or financial investment and prohibition of official contacts for periods ranging from a few months up to a couple of years. Hu Jintao undoubtedly continues to have an influential voice on matters relating to Tibet.

Chen Kuiyuan (November 1992 – October 2000): Chen Kuiyuan today is 71 years of age. He belongs to Liaoning Province and spent the first 32 years of his career in Inner Mongolia. He considers himself a Marxist Leninist theoretician and is an authority on Tang poetry. As Party Secretary in Tibet, he relied heavily on the counsel and advice of his most powerful Tibetan Deputy Party Secretary, Raidi. Following the period of martial law in 1989, law and order policies were the order of the day while officialdom struggled to reestablish authority.

After his tenure in TAR, Chen Kuiyuan spent two years as Party Secretary in Henan Province before being posted to Beijing as the Party Secretary and Head of the Chinese Academy of Social Sciences (CASS). Here his Maoist theoretical talents blossomed. Hu Jintao had started his stewardship with an even emphasis on the concepts of stability, reform and development. He then personally added to this his own contributions of a 'harmonious society' and a 'scientific society,' but thanks to Chen Kuiyuan who prolifically produced theoretical papers at CASS, by 2002, this original balance of ideas gradually gave way to Chen Kuiyuan's calls for adherence to 'Deng Xiaoping's Four Basic Principles' and the all-out promotion of 'safeguarding stability' (wei-hu wen-ding 维护稳定) reflected in the slogan 'Stability Above All Else' (稳定压倒一切). These latter 'wei-wen' stability concepts tended to rely heavily on the use of force to the exclusion of reform. Chen Kuiyuan spent more than a decade as leader of CASS. He continues to keep closely monitoring Tibetan issues, presumably by vetting the research on Tibet carried out by CASS scholars and through contacts with the Tibet Academy of Social Sciences in Lhasa. The Tibet Academy of Social Sciences is headed by Padma Lhagyal, younger brother of Padma Choling the third ranked TAR official in Tibet. Chen Kuiyuan had a long tenure as Politburo member and was again a delegate to the 18th Party Congress. He retired in 2013, but continues to use his academic and high level intra-Party channels to foster his conservative views of development in Tibet.

Guo Jinlong (October 2000 – December 2004): Guo Jinlong is a 65-year old native of Nanjing. His early career was in Sichuan where between 1969 and 1993 he rose from county and prefectural positions to attain a Deputy Party Secretary position in the province. He then was assigned to the TAR where from 1994 to 2000 he continued at the Deputy Party Secretary level. In October 2000, he replaced Chen Kuiyuan as TAR Party Secretary. During his four year stint as TAR Party Secretary, Guo Jinlong focused heavily on policies to stimulate economic development. His term also was largely free of political and ethnic disturbances. His next assignment was as Party Secretary in Anhui Province for three years followed by a posting to Beijing as Mayor at the end of 2007.

His patron Hu Jintao had him promoted as Party Secretary of Beijing in July 2012. Guo Jinlong was made a member of the CCP CC Politburo at the 18th Party Congress and was expected to provide encouragement to then TAR Party Secretary Chen Quanguo who copied a number of Guo Jinlong's earlier economic priorities.

Yang Chuantang (December 2004 – November 2005): Yang Chuantang is from Shandong and was born in 1954. His early career was in the Communist Youth League (primarily in Shandong) and he joined the CCP in 1976. He arrived in Tibet in 1993 and spent ten years there working his way up to the Deputy Party Secretary-level before being transferred north to Qinghai as its Governor. In 2004 Yang Chuantang returned to Tibet as Party Secretary but lasted only a year because of a sudden, severe heart attack or stroke. This terminated any plans for him to continue working in the Qinghai-Tibet Plateau.

Following his recovery, Hu Jintao made certain that Yang Chuantang received one important assignment after another in Beijing. First he was appointed Party Secretary of the Nationalities Affairs Commission under the State Council. Next he became Party Secretary of the China Federation of Supply & Marketing Cooperatives, and later Yang Chuantang was named Party Secretary and Minister of the Communications and Transport Ministry. This was particularly interesting since there were rumours that the scandal-plagued Railway Ministry would be merged with Communications and Transport to form a super Ministry. This was a sure indication that Hu Jintao had confidence in Yang Chuantang and knew that he could count on his future support. Once the merger materialized, Yang Chuantang had an important hand in finalising the railroad extensions in Tibet, including the spur to Nepal and the spurs to Nyingtri and Yatong alongthe Indian border. Yang Chuantang is a full member of the 18th Central Committee.

Zhang Qingli (November 2005 – August 2011): In China, Zhang Qingli is routinely referred to as the 'Iron Party Secretary.' (铁腕书记). 'Tie-wan 'means 'iron wrist,' not 'iron fist.' The word 'wrist' suggests a decisive decision-maker who is clever, tough and stubborn, not someone who can govern only by brute force.

A study of his daily movements while he was in Tibet showed that Zhang Qingli was probably the most pro-active of recent Party Secretaries. Despite suffering from high blood pressure and frequent bouts of altitude sickness which, among other things, prevented proper sleep at night, he carried on travelling non-stop to just about every one of Tibet's 72 counties and presided over the massive infrastructure construction that characterized his 5½ years at the helm.

In August 2011 Zhang Qingli was rewarded and transferred to Hebei Province as its Party Secretary. To repeat the Qing Dynasty Prime Minister, Li Hongzhang's description of Vietnam and Korea being the lips protecting China's teeth, Zhang Qingli's Hebei Province plays the same lips-to-teeth function for Beijing Municipality today. Instead of foreign invaders however, Hebei must protect access to China's political capital from grievance petitioners and dissidents.

Zhang Qingli is now 64 years old and a full member of the 18th CCP Central Committee, but he was not promoted to the Politburo. He has, however, been appointed to a position of national importance and appointed Secretary General of the 12th CPPCC, in which capacity he continues to have a formal role in the CCP's polcies towards the ethnic minorities and especially Tibetans. .

What is interesting is that in the first week from the date of the 18th Party Congress being announced, the website of the Chinese Communist Party in Beijing published two positive stories on Zhang Qingli, one including a large photograph. This seemed to indicate that Zhang Qingli retains the support and confidence of the Party leadership. There is little doubt that Zhang Qingli will be involved in future Tibet policy formulation and the leadership will use him as at least as one of their points of reference.

Chen Quanquo (August 2011 – August, 2016): Chen Quanguo, a Han Chinese born in 1955 in Pingyu in Henan Province, joined the CCP in 1976. A Postgraduate from Wuhan Automotive Polytechnic University, he graduated from the Economics Department of Zhengzhou University with a Masters in Economics.

Chen Quanguo brought to Tibet a more easy going political style than his predecessor. His first year was, possibly as a result, surprisingly crisis-free. He has concentrated on issues like health care, housing and job creation for new Tibetan graduates. There is some suspicion that most of the new jobs entail listening to and transcribing overseas telephone communications of TAR citizens. Chen Quanguo also implemented the restrictive 'grid' security and 'Skynet' surveillance systems which, as confirmed by Losang Gyaltsen in November 2012, have divided the TAR into a closely monitored grid to ensure that teams of security personnel can be mobilised within two minutes. This was accompanied by a hugely ambitious and massively intrusive policy of placing small government work teams in every one of the TAR's 5,453 villages for a five year period. While Chen Quanguo did not conceive this policy, he was charged with implementing it. He simultaneously began rigorously implementing policies to promote Han-Tibetan inter-ethnic marriages, installation of CCP Cadres in monasteries and co-opting of abbots and monks to work for the CCP by instituting a system of rewards and benefits and awards to 'patriotic monks'.

Chen Quanguo is a full member of the 18th CCP Central Committee. While some reports indicate that Li Keqiang was one of his patrons, other credible reports assert that he was appointed TAR Party Secretary at Xi Jinping's specific behest. His transfer as Party Secretary of the troubled Xinjiang-Uyghur Autonomous Region, confirms that his tenure in Tibet has been appreciated and he will probably be promoted to the Poliburo at the 19th Party Congress in late 2017. He was replaced on 28th August, 2016 by Wu Yingjie.

Wu Yingjie (August 2016 --): Born in Changyi County in Shandong Province in December 1956, Wu Yingjie graduated from a high school in Shandong in 1974. He has an impeccable 'Red' pedigree. His father, Wu Ziming was a member of the Party committee and Secretary of the Communist Youth League of Changyi County, Shandong Province. Wu Ziming was transferred to Tibet from Shandong's Changyi county in 1956, before Wu Yingjie was born, and assigned work in Golmud. All his family members along with Wu Yingjie came to settle with him in Golmud in 1958.

It would be difficult for the CCP to find another ethnic Han cadre who is as 'Tibetan' as Wu Yingjie. The last Han cadre fluent in Tibetan and who was regarded as a 'Tibetan' was former PLA Lt. General Yin Fatang, who served as Party Secretary of TAR from 1980-1985.

Till his elevation Wu Yingjie was one of four TAR Deputy Party Secretaries, with the others being Padma Choling (Tib), Lobsang Gyaltsen (Tib) and Deng Xiaogang (Han). While Padma Choling and Lobsang Gyaltsen were ranked higher, Wu Yingje was designated the Executive Deputy Secretary. An indication that Wu Yingjie was earmarked for promotion was his being sent to attend the Central Party School in Beijing from March 2000 to January 2001. He studied in the CCP Central Party School's Research Institute, focusing particularly on Party history.

Wu Yingjie first came to TAR as an "educated youth" under the Tibet Aid programme and worked in Nyingchi. In October 1977, he came to live in Lhasa and became a worker at a power plant in the western part of the region. He stayed on in Tibet for over 40 years and joined the CCP in May 1978. Three years after the Chinese government resumed the all-China college entrance exam, Wu Yingjie enrolled in the Chinese Language and Literature Department of the Tibet Nationalities Institute, Xianyang in Shaanxi in 1979.

After graduating from University in August 1983, he was assigned the post of clerk in the Board of Education of the TAR. In 1986, Wu Yingjie was promoted to Senior Staff and in April 1987 was appointed the Deputy Director of the Primary and Secondary Education Department of the Tibet Autonomous Region Science and Technology Education Commission. Through the 1990s, he held the posts of Deputy Director as well as Director of the Assistance Office and was later promoted as Deputy Director of the Board of Education in the Tibet Autonomous Region Board of Education. By the time he was 43 years old (May 2000), Wu Yingjie was appointed the Director of the Tibet Education Department. Credible reports state that during his tenure in the TAR Board of Education, Wu Yingjie "worked hard to promote the development of education in Tibet" and made "important contributions" to the Tibetan schools.

In January 2003, Wu Yingjie, was promoted to the level of a Deputy Provincial cadre and appointed Vice Chairman of the TAR Government. Thereon Wu Yingjie served in the TAR Party Committee as Director of the TAR Party Propaganda Department and later as Deputy Chairman of the TAR Government. In November 2011, Wu Yingjie was appointed Deputy Party Secretary of the Autonomous Region, Deputy Chairman of the Autonomous Region Government Executive and Deputy Secretary of the leading group of the Party. In April 2013, he succeeded Hao Peng as Governor of Qinghai Province and was concurrently Deputy Chairman of the Autonomous Region Government's Executive.

As Director of the TAR Propaganda Department, Wu Yingjie received special credit for the propaganda work during the TAR's 40th anniversary celebrations in 2005. The Region's propaganda work was praised as "smooth and fast". At the time of the March riots in Lhasa in 2008, he would have worked closely with Liu Yunshun, then Director of the CCP CC's Propaganda Department, in shaping a decisive role for the CCP's propaganda apparatus which for the first time introduced a schism between the Han majority and Tibetans. Liu Yunshun is currently a Member of the PBSC. Official Chinese media reports state that "a resounding success of patriotism education was seen" during Wu Yingjie's tenure as Director of the TAR's Propaganda Department.

Some interesting remarks have been made by Wu Yingjie in the past. When meeting a group of seven South Asian journalists including four from India (hosted by China's State Council Information Office) on a tour to showcase developments in Tibet, TAR Deputy Secretary Wu Yingjie disclosed to the journalists in Lhasa on August 25, 2014, that talks were on with the Dalai Lama. He clarified that these were being held through "personal envoys" and limited to discussing the possibility of his return to Tibet. He said, "All Tibetans, including the Dalai Lama and the people around him, can return if they accept Tibet and Taiwan as part of China, and give up 'splittist' efforts."

Also, in October 2009, Wu Yingjie told US diplomats travelling in Tibet that the Dalai Lama and his "clique" masterminded the "March 14" incident the previous year as part of a bid to take back feudal power in Tibet.

Wu Yingjie also asserted that "the "Dalai" uses his religious role for political purposes and that the "March 14th Incident" was masterminded by the Dalai in order to destroy the Beijing Olympics. The Dalai just doesn't want to lose his power". He added that "In the old days, five percent of the people controlled 95 percent of the land. The Dalai wants to restore his feudal rule, but the serfs have already been liberated. America freed all the black slaves and people welcomed that, but China freed all the Tibetan slaves under the "Dalai Clique," and some people are not happy". Wu Yingjie added "I don't know why." He said "some foreign countries also give money to the Dalai and send high-level delegations to Dharamsala. For example, U.S. Speaker of the House Pelosi and a White House senior staff member special emissary both went to Dharamsala to see the Dalai Lama".

He said "The Dalai is asking China to withdraw its People's Liberation Army (PLA), and other non-Tibetan people from the region, and is trying to create a so-called "Greater Tibet" that would include ethnic Tibetan areas of

Sichuan, Qinghai, Yunnan and Gansu. No sovereign state could accept such demands, which would divide the country".

He claimed that during the 11th Five-Year Plan the TAR had invested a lot of money in restoring religious sites and protecting Tibetan culture and the many people praying at temples in Lhasa testify to the government's protection of religious freedom. Wu Yingjie also said "Nearly all rural Tibetans can read, however, one-quarter of Tibetans still live without electric power" and that "Tibetans are not economically marginalized and discrimination based on ethnic background is illegal".

Wu Yingjie disclosed too that "After the March 14th (2008) incident, 950 people were arrested and 80 of them were sentenced... Two hundred monks from outside of the TAR who were in the TAR without legal documents were sent back to their home areas, but no monks or nuns are missing. The government views the monasteries as public units (*gonggong danwei*). Therefore, the government provides the monasteries with free medical care, drinking water, and electricity, and also builds and maintains roads to the monasteries". He also said that "During the 11th Five Year Plan the TAR has invested considerable money in the protection of Tibetan culture. For example, the government invested 380 million RMB in repairs of the Potala Palace, and the Sakya, Norbulinka, and Tashi Lhunpo Monasteries". He said the government had built many hospitals of traditional Tibetan medicine and protected about 100 kinds of Tibetan customs as part of the PRC's "national intangible cultural heritage."

Wu Yingjie said "over 98 percent of rural youth and middle aged people are literate -- that is, they are able to read the Tibetan language edition of the Tibet Daily. The government also sends many Tibetan students to inland China to study for free. Generous stipends are provided to students from the TAR who are accepted into a university in inland China".

Dismissing remarks that Tibetans were being discriminated against, he pointed out that in TAR, 70 percent of the civil servants are ethnic minorities and only 30 percent are ethnic Han.

Wu Yingjie is reputed to get along well with colleagues and be good at delegating work. He is 1.83 metres, or just over six feet, tall and a good athlete who has played basketball and volleyball.

Wu Yingjie's appointment suggests an effort by Beijing to adopt a more 'sensitive' and understanding approach towards Tibetans. While his predecessor Chen Quanguo focussed more on tightening security and enhancing the Party's presence and surveillance throughout Tibet, Wu Yingjie is likely to give more importance to the TAR's propaganda effort and retain the focus on education.

United Front Work Department (UFWD)

The CCP CC's United Front Work Department (UFWD) looks after matters relating to China's 55 ethnic minority nationalities and non-CCP entities, including Hongkong and Taiwan. The organization plays a central role in Tibetan affairs.

SUN CHUNLAN (f)

She was appointed Director of the CCP CC UFWD on December 31, 2014, following Ling Jihua's removal on charges of misuse of authority. 64-year old Sun Chunlan was earlier Party Secretary of Tianjin.

Born: May 1950, Hebei Province.

Education: Sun Chunlan graduated from the Anshan Industrial Technology Academy in Liaoning province in 1969.

Ethnicity: Han Chinese

Career: She spent 36 years in various official positions in Liaoning, including as Party chief of the provincial capital Dalian, before being moved to Beijing to take up the role of Deputy Chief of the All China Federation of Trade Unions in November 2005.

In 2007, Sun Chunlan was elected to the CCP's Central Committee as a full member. In late 2009, she was "parachuted" into Fujian province as Party Secretary, where she remained until November 2012, when she was reassigned to Tianjin.

Her career profile strongly suggests proximity to CCP CC General Secretary Xi Jinping and his predecessor, Hu Jintao.

She is likely to retire at the forthcoming 19th Party Congress in late 2017.

ZHANG YIJIONG

Born: 1955, Shanghai

Education: Worked in a Qinghai factory in 1972. Graduate of the Central Party School.

Ethnicity: Han Chinese

Career: Formerly a member of the Communist Youth League (CYL) (1985-1990). He spent most of his career in Qinghai and the Tibet Autonomous Region (TAR), which served as a training ground for the United Front Work Department. A former Deputy Party Secretary of the TAR (2006-2010), he is a potential interlocutor for the Tibetan Government in exile.

Current Designation: Executive Vice Director of the CCP CC's UFWD and Member of 18th CCP Central Committee.

ZHU WEIQUN

Born: 1947, Jiangsu Province

Education: People's University, Beijing and Masters in Journalism from the Chinese Academy of Social Sciences (CASS).

Ethnicity: Han Chinese

Current Designation: Chairman of the Committee for Ethnic and Religious Affairs of the National Committee of the Chinese People's Political Consultative Conference (CPPCC). In February 2012, Zhu Weiqun attracted international media with an article in the Party's 'Study Times' journal which said that listing ethnic minority status on identity cards, using ethnic names for schools and regions and reserving privileges for ethnic minorities were obstacles to nationalism and cohesion. He was earlier the Executive Vice Director of the United Front Work Department (UFWD)'s Tibet Section and spokesperson for Tibet affairs in the past.

Regarded a 'hardliner' on issues relating to Tibet, he continues to regularly intervene and have a major say on issues related to Tibet and Tibetans. At the fourth session of the 12th NPC in March 2015, he criticised the Dalai Lama for suggesting that he might discontinue the institution of Dalai Lama and insisted on its continuance while asserting that Beijing alone has the right to recognise 'reincarnations' of high lamas. He was instrumental in getting a list finalised of the Chinese government-approved 870 'living Buddhas' in January 2016. Zhu Weiqun was also quoted by China's official media on June 26, 2017 when China stopped Indian pilgrims from travelling through Nathu La to Kailash Mansarovar.

He remained as the No.2 ranked Vice Minister (accorded full Minister rank) in the UFWD with Zhang Yijiong ranked at No.3 below him. Zhu Weiqun also acted as the chief personal escort of Standing Committee member Li Changchun during his much publicized trip to Tibet in August 2012 and followed that up with an anniversary commemoration visit to Labrang Monastery in Gansu. During the visit the official Chinese media identified Zhu Weiqun by a title he has held for years but has been seldom used previously i.e. Secretary General of the Central Tibet Working Coordination Small Group. He also accompanied CPPCC Chairman Yu Zhengsheng during his trip to Tibetan areas in Sichuan in February 2013.

SITHAR

Born: 1953 in Dege, Sichuan (Eastern Tibet)

Education: Graduated from a Teacher's College and has a Masters in Philosophy.

Ethnicity: Tibetan

Current Designation: Head of the 7th Bureau, UFWD which was established in 2005 to deal with Tibetan affairs. He joined UFWD in 1984. He was appointed in October 2010. In the past, he has interacted with the Tibetan Government in Exile in the 1980s. He is also known by the name "Dralha".

Chinese Communist Party in TAR

The Chinese Communist Party (CCP) Committee of the Tibet Autonomous Region (TAR) is headed by a Secretary, who is assisted by five Deputy Secretaries. The Standing Committee manages the routine business. Party Committees are elected every five years at the TAR, Administrative District (AD) and Municipality levels and every three years at lower administrative and production units. There are presently more than 2,25,200 Chinese Communist Party (CCP) members in TAR. There are 185,800 cadres belonging to ethnic minority nationalities working in TAR of whom 37,000 are cadres of Tibetan nationality in TAR. Women cadres occupy 30 percent of the posts at the Autonomous Region level.

WU YINGJIE

Year of Birth: December 1956, Changyi County of Shandong Province.

Ethnicity: Han Chinese

Education: Graduation and post-graduation in History from Central Party School. Worked in Central Party School in October 1974.

He joined the CCP in May 1987. His recent posts were Vice-Chairman and Standing Committee member of the TAR People's Government from November 2011-December 2012. He was also a Deputy Secretary of the TAR Party Committee and a member of TAR Party Standing Committee till August, 2016. He was elevated to the post TAR Party Secretary on August 28, 2016.

For more details about Wu, refer to pages 19-23.

Deputy Secretaries of TAR Party Committee

PEMA CHOLING/PEMA TRINLEY/PADMA CHOLING

Ethnicity: Tibetan

Year of Birth: in October 1952, Chamdo Prefecture

Education: Joined PLA at the age of 17 from Qinghai Province. He served in the PLA for seventeen years. He mastered the Chinese language while serving in the PLA.

Current Designation: Chairman of TAR People's Congress. He assumed office on January 15, 2010. He is one of the most senior ethnic Tibetans in TAR politics and the longest serving Chinese Communist Party member in TAR.

Pema Choling was promoted to the 18th CCP CC in 2012 after serving in the CCP for more than three decades. He is believed to be a "hardliner" and has issued provocative statements in the past. In January 2010, he said that the "fight against the Dalai Lama clique is meant to be lasting, intense, complicated, and sometimes fought vehemently." In March 2010 he revealed that the Panchen Lama now 20 years old, is still living in Tibet: "As far as I know, his family and he are now living a very good life in Tibet. He and his family are reluctant to be disturbed. They want to live an ordinary life." He claims to be close to the 17th Karmapa, Ugyen Trinley Dorje and has said they are "mates from the same hometown." He has stated in the past and again at the fourth session of the 12th NPC that the reincarnation of the XIVth Dalai Lama needs Beijing's approval and the Dalai Lama must not discontinue the institution of the Dalai Lama and tamper with traditional Tibetan Buddhist practices.

He is described as "stern but amiable." He is fond of playing basket ball.

LOBSANG GYALTSEN/LOSANG JAMCAN

Year of Birth: 1957, Dakyab (Ch: Zhag'yab) County of Chamdo Prefecture.

Ethnicity: Tibetan

Education: He entered the work force in 1976 and joined the CCP in 1978. Lobsang studied at the Literature Department of Tibet Nationality College from 1971 to 1976, and graduated from the Central Party School with a postgraduate degree in 2004. He taught Marxist Theory at the University for 10 years.

Career: Between 1995-2003, Lobsang Gyaltsen served as Deputy Secretary of the CCP Lhasa City Committee; Vice-Mayor, Acting Mayor and Mayor of Lhasa City of TAR.

Current Designation: He was appointed Chairman of the TAR People's Government in January 2013 - a position traditionally held by Han Chinese. He reports directly to Tibet's top official i.e TAR Party Secretary Wu Yingjie. He is a hardcore Communist and believes that unity of the motherland, harmony, and stability are the basic guarantees of Tibet's development and prosperity. He is an Alternate Member of the 18^{th}CCP CC.

A Khampa from Dragyab in Chamdo, Lobsang Gyaltsen is described by people who have met him as a dour, humourless person and an ideologue.

DENG XIAOGANG

Year of Birth: August 1967, Guiyang County of Hunan Province.

Ethnicity: Han Chinese

Education: Graduated from Hunan Agricultural University and holds a Ph.D in economics.

Career: Deng Xiaogang, joined the CCP in 1991, and entered the work force in 1992. He has served as Vice-Chairman and Assistant Chairman of the TAR People's Government. From 2012 till date he has overseen the TAR's security apparatus as Secretary of the TAR Politics and Law Committee. He visited and stayed in Ngari (Ch: Ali) for almost two months and inspected border Security and PLA army bases.

Current Designation: Deputy Secretary of TAR Party Committee since 2013. As the Secretary of the Politics and Law Committee of TAR, he is responsible for the law and order, security apparatus and police in Tibet. He accompanied Wang Jianping, Commander of the People's Armed Police Force (PAPF) during his tour of Tibet in June 2014.

Members of the Standing Committee of TAR Party Committee

WU YINGJIE
Ethnicity: Han Chinese

PEMA TRINLEY/PEMA CHOLING
Ethnicity: Tibetan

DENG XIAOGANG
Ethnicity: Han Chinese

LOBSANG GYALTSEN (Ch: LOSANG JAMCAN)
Ethnicity: Tibetan

(See Page 27, 28, 29 and 30 for their bio details)

Lt General **DIAO GUOXIN**

Year of Birth: October 1958 in Taixing county, Jiangsu province.

Ethnicity: Han Chinese

Year of Joining PLA: February 1976

Current Designation: Member of the TAR Party Committee and Political Commissar of Tibet Military District.

Diao Guoxin enlisted in the PLA in February 1976, and joined the Communist Party of China in March 1979. He is a university graduate.

In February 1979, Diao was transferred from the Nanjing Military Region to the 14th Group Army, and fought in the Sino-Vietnamese War. He also fought in the Battle of Koulinshan in May 1981 and the Battle of Laoshan in April 1984, during the subsequent Sino-Vietnamese conflicts. He was twice awarded for military valour

He was promoted as Lieutenant General on July 15, 2014.

Dropped from TAR Party Standing Committee in late 2016 as part of ongoing PLA reforms.

CHOEDAK/CHEDAK

Year of Birth: August 1958, Shangri-la of Yunnan Province

Year of Joining CCP: May 1982.

Ethnicity: Tibetan

Current Designation: He is currently a member of the Standing Committee of the TAR Party Committee and Chairman of the TAR's United Front Work Department and Party Secretary of Lhasa Municipality.

Current Designation: Member of Standing Committee of TAR Party Committee, President of TAR People's Higher Court and Party Secretary of Communist Party of Chamdo (Ch: Qamdo), Choedak is a 58 year old Tibetan from Gyalthang (Zhongdian, Yunnan Province). In 1979 he started his career as a Communist Youth League (CYL) worker which led to an educational administration position as head of the Gyalthang Party School. This was followed by a number of years in propaganda assignments. He was appointed Party Secretary of Gyalthang County in 1994, chief government administrator of Dechen Tibetan Prefecture in 2001 (the year Zhongdian County changed its name to 'Shangri-la' County) and finally Party Secretary of Dechen in 2007. In 2010 he was elevated to the Yunnan Province Communist Party Standing Committee and, shortly thereafter, was transferred to Tibet where he was given a slot on the Tibet Autonomous Region (TAR) Party Standing Committee and initially took responsibility for the TAR United Front Department portfolio. In late 2011, Chodak was appointed Lhasa Party Secretary replacing the Han Chinese Qin Yizhi (who had left Tibet to head China's Communist Youth League from its headquarters in Beijing). As Lhasa Party Secretary, Choedak is the most powerful official in Lhasa municipal politics which covers the city and seven surrounding counties. He represents this large area on the TAR Party Standing Committee where he ranks 8th as an ordinary member.

NORBU DHONDUP

Year of Birth: December 1960 in Gongyai county of Lhoka (Ch: Shannan)

Ethnicity: Tibetan

Year of joining CCP: June 1978 and started working for the Party in August 1978.

Education: He graduated from the Central Party School.

Current Designation: Member of Standing Committee of TAR Party Committee, President of TAR People's Higher Court and Party Secretary of Communist Party of Chamdo (Ch: Qamdo)

GONPO TASHI

Born: October 1962; Palung county of Amdo (Ch: Haulong in Qinghai

Ethnicity: Tibetan

Year of Joining CCP: July 1983 and started working for the Party in July 1978

Education: Is a graduate

Previous Designation: Chairman of TAR United Front Work Department (UFWD) and Secretary of TAR PPCC from November 2011 to January 2012.

Current Designation: Chairman of TAR UFWD, Deputy Chairman and Secretary of TAR PPCC since January 2012.

DONG YUNHU

Year of birth: December 1962 in Zhejiang Province

Ethnicity: Han Chinese

Year of Joining CCP: April 1985 and started working for the Party in July 1986. He is a Professor of Philosophy.

Education: Has a graduate degree in Philosophy.

Current Designation: member of the TAR Party Standing Committee and Chairman of TAR Propaganda Department since December 2011.

LANG TIANGENG

Year of Birth: May 1960, Hongmao County of Guangdong Province of China

Ethnicity: Han Chinese

Education: He holds a Doctorate degree in Agriculture.

He joined the CCP in September 1976 before completing his Doctorate degree in 1984. He worked in various capacities including that of Deputy Director of the Economic Restructuring Committee of Guizhou Province, Deputy Director of the Ministry of Agriculture, Personnel and Labor Secretary of PRC's Agricultural Ministry etc. He was a member of TAR Party Committee from March-April 2012

Current Designation: He was appointed member of the TAR Party Standing Committee in April 2012. He is currently also a Standing Committee member of the TAR Party Organization Department.

DOTO

Year of Birth: 1959 in Palgon County (Ch: Baingoin) of Nagchu (Ch: Nagqu) Prefecture

Ethnicity: Tibetan

Education: Graduated from Central University Nationalities Politics Department in Political Theory and Political Economics (July 1982-September 1984).

Year of Joining CCP: 1984.

Current Designation: He is currently a member of the TAR Party Committee and Vice-Chairman of Nagchu (Ch: Nagqu) Party Committee. He was replaced by Gao Yang as the Party Secretary of Nagchu Prefecture in 2014.

DING YINXIAN

Year of Birth: October 1960 in Yanggu County of Shandong.

Ethnicity: Han Chinese

Education: Completed graduation in Computer Engineering from Shandong Province School of Electronics Industry. Holds a Ph.D. He initially worked in Lhoka (Ch: Shannan) Administrative District as deputy Chief and Chief of Industrial Power and Electricity Control Authority in late 1980s and mid 1990s. He was Assistant Chairman of TAR People's Government.

Current Designation: He was appointed a member of the TAR Party Standing Committee and Vice-Chairman of TAR People's Government in July 2013.

WANG RUILIAN

Year of Birth: 1964, Haidong prefecture of western Qinghai Province.

Ethnicity: Han Chinese

He joined the CCP in 1985. He had worked earlier in various positions in Tibet. He worked as the Party Secretary of Chamdo Prefectural Committee and Chairman of the Chamdo People's Congress from 2008-2011. He worked as Secretary General of TAR Party Committee from 2011-2012.

Current Designation: Vice Chairman of TAR People's Congress and Standing Committee member of TAR Party Committee.

TAR People's Government

The TAR People's Government is headed by a Chairman, who concurrently holds the post of Deputy Secretary in the TAR Party Committee, assisted by 12 Vice Chairmen and a Secretary General. There are six Commissions and a number of Departments, all with headquarters in Lhasa. There are a total of 15 members including the Chairman. The TAR People's Government consists of 8 Tibetans and 7 Han Chinese members.

CHAIRMAN: LOBSANG GYALTSEN/LOSANG JAMCAN

Ethnicity: Tibetan

(See page 29 for his Bio-details)

ZHUANGYAN WEI, a Han, born in August 1967 and who has a Master's Degree in Economics, was in mid-2017 appointed Vice Chairman of the TAR People's Government. Prior to this he was, and still is, Deputy Secretary of the TAR Party Committee, Deputy Secretary of the Party Group of the District Government, and Dean of the School of Administrative Affairs of TAR. He had previously served in the Jilin Provincial Party Committee in positions such as Vice Governor, the Propaganda Department, as well as the Jilin Provincial Standing Committee until his transfer to Tibet. He replaced Ding Yinxian, Deputy Chairman of TAR People's Government who was appointed a member of the TAR Party Standing Committee and Vice-Chairman of TAR People's Government in July 2013.

VICE CHAIRMEN OF TAR PEOPLE'S GOVERNMENT

DENG XIAOGANG

Ethnicity: Han Chinese

DING YINXIAN

Han Chinese

(For their Bio-details, see Pages 29 and 35 respectively)

CHAKRA LOBSANG TENZIN

Year of Birth: December, 1953 in Lhasa

Ethnicity: Tibetan

Education: Has a graduate degree

Current Designation: Vice-Chairman of TAR People's Government. He started working for the CCP ever since he was recognized as a Tulku of Jampaling Monastery of Chamdo in November 1956.

MENG DELI

Year of Birth: March 1955 in Jingyang County of Shaanxi Province

Ethnicity: Han Chinese

Education: Is a graduate of the Central Party School.

Year of Joining CCP: June 1983. He served in the PLA from 1973-1976

Current Designation: Vice-Chairman of the TAR People's Government since January 2008 and Secretary of TAR Education Committee since October 2011.

DEKYI (f)

Year of Birth: June 1959 in Zogang County of Chamdo Prefecture

Ethnicity: Tibetan

Year of Joining CCP: September 1984

Education: Completed Post graduation in 1977

Current Designations: Vice-Chairman of TAR People's Government and Chairman of TAR Red Cross.

KELSANG TSERING

Year of Birth: December 1955 in Amdo County of Nagchu (Ch: Nagqu)

Ethnicity: Tibetan

Year of Joining CCP: December 1974

Education: Professional training in Tibetan Language Translation from Central Institute for National Minority Languages and Literature Department.

Current Designation: Vice-Chairman of TAR People's Government.

GYALTSEN

Year of Birth: December 1962; Naidong County of Lhoka (Ch: Shannan)

Ethnicity: Tibetan

Year of Joining CCP: November 1984

Education: Graduated in Finance from the Central Party School

Current Designation: Vice-Chairman of TAR People's Government.

DORJEE TSEDUP

Year of Birth: June 1962; Rutog County of Ngari (Ch: Ali)

Ethnicity: Tibetan

Year of Joining CCP: April 1983

Education: Completed Post graduation in January 1980

Previous Designation: Mayor of Lhasa (January 2007- December 2012).

Current Designation: Vice-Chairman of TAR People's Government, Director of the 7th Advisory Inspectorate; Regional Party Committee; Deputy Director of Autonomous Region Stability Maintenance Advisory Inspectorate

DUNG MINGJUN

Year of Birth: May 1962 in Shouguang County of Shandong Province, China

Ethnicity: Han Chinese

Year of Joining CCP: July 1983

Education: Completed graduation in Architecture from Shandong Mining Institute

Current Designation: Vice-Chairman of TAR People's Government

PENPA TASHI

Ethnicity: Tibetan

Year of Birth: October 1964 in Lhozhag County of Lhoka (Ch: Shannan)

Education: Completed graduation in Law from Renmin University, Beijing in July 1988

Current Designation: Vice-Chairman of TAR People's Government.

ZENG MINGWAN

Year of birth: January 1964 in Chengdu of Sichuan Province

Ethnicity: Han Chinese

Education: A PhD graduate from Southwest University of Finance and Economics.

Year of Joining CCP: December 1987

Current Designation: He was appointed as the Vice Chairman of TAR People's Government during the seventh meeting of TAR People's Congress on November 26, 2013.

JIANG JIE

Year of Birth: October 1965; Jiaozhou County of Shandong Province

Ethnicity: Han Chinese

Year of Joining CCP: April 1985

Education: Completed his PhD in Management from Shandong University

Previous Designation: Chairman of Shandong Municipal People's Congress and Shandong Party School.

Current Designation: He was appointed Vice Chairman of TAR People's Government in July 2013.

HE WENHAO

Ethnicity: Han Chinese

Previous Designation: Deputy Secretary and member of Standing Committee of Ningxia Hui Autonomous Region Party Committee and Director of the National Security Office of the same region.

Current Designation: He was appointed as the Vice Chairman of TAR People's Government during the seventh meeting of TAR People's Congress on 26 November, 2013.

XUXUE GUANG

Year of Birth: November 1958

Ethnicity: Han Chinese

Education: Graduate of the Tibet Nationalities Institute

Previous Designation: Deputy Secretary of Shigatse (Ch: Xigaze) Party Committee, Commissioner of the Administrative Office of Shigatse and Deputy Secretary of TAR People's Government.

Current Designation: Deputy Secretary and Secretary General of TAR People's Government since January 2013.

TAR People's Political Consultative Conference (CPPCC) Committee

The TAR CPPCC is headed by a Chairman, who is assisted by 16 Vice Chairmen, a Secretary General and a 52-member Standing Committee.

PPCC CHAIRMAN- PHAKPA LHA GELEK NAMGYAL

Ethnicity: Tibetan

Year of Birth: February 1940 in Lithang, eastern Part of Tibet in West Sichuan province. He was recognized as the reincarnation of the 11th Pagbhalha Huthok Tulku of Jampaling Monastery in Chamdo at the age of two in September 1942.

Year of joining CCP: September 1950 as the first Deputy Director of Chamdo Liberation Committee.

Education: Completed his graduation in September 1950.

Current Designation: Member of the 12th Chinese People's Political Consultative Conference (CPPCC); Chairman of TAR PPCC and Vice President of the Buddhist Association of China since 2002.

Vice Chairmen of TAR People's Political Consultative Conference (PPCC) Committee

GONPO TASHI

Year of Birth: October 1962 in Palung county of Amdo (Ch: Haulong) in Qinghai

Ethnicity: Tibetan

Year of Joining CCP: July 1983; started working for the Party in July 1978

Education: Has a graduate degree

Current Designation: Member Standing Committee of TAR Party Committee, Deputy Chairman of TAR PPCC and Secretary of TAR UFWD.

DHUPKHANG THUPKHE

Year of Birth: December 1955 in Nagchu (Ch: Nagqu) He was also recognized as the reincarnation of Dhupkhang Tulku in Shabten Monastery of Nagchu County at the age of 3.

Ethnicity: Tibetan

Education: Completed graduation

Year of Joining CCP: July1980

Current Designation: Vice-Chairman of TAR PPCC, President of China Buddhist Association Tibet Branch.

TSE MONLING TENZIN TRINLAY

Year of Birth: September 1950 in Lhasa

Ethnicity: Tibetan

Year of Joining CCP: 1956

Education: He was recognized as the reincarnation of the 5thTsemoling. He studied Buddhist scriptures in Sera Monastery and sociology from a primary school in Lhasa.

Current Designation: He is a Vice Chairman of TAR PPCC. He has been the Vice-President of Buddhist Association of China several times.

JUNGLO JAMPA KHEDUP

Year of Birth: August 1940 in Chamdo Prefecture. He was recognized as a Tulku of Riwoche Monastery of Chamdo in November 1943. He studied Buddhist scriptures and texts from Zonglo Monastery in Chamdo.

Ethnicity: Tibetan

Year of Joining CCP: November 1997

Education: Completed till high School

Current Designation: Vice-Chairman of TAR PPCC, Vice-Chairman of Chamdo Prefectural Committee, Chairman of Buddhist Association of Chamdo and Chairman of Jampaling Monastery of Chamdo's Temple Management Committee

SALUNG PHUNLHAK

Year of Birth: March 1943 in Shigatse (Ch: Xigaze)

Ethnicity: Tibetan

Year of Joining CCP: July 1982

Education: Completed high school

Current Designation: Vice Chairman of TAR PPCC and the first Director of Tashilunpo Monastery's Temple Management Committee.

JINSHI XIAN

Year of Birth: 1955 in Beijing

Ethnicity: Han Chinese

Year of Joining CCP: 1981

Education: Completed Post graduation in Engineering from Shanghai Railway University on January 1982

Current Designation: Vice-Chairman of TAR PPCC and Director of TAR District Development and Reform Commission.

GAO YANG

Year of Birth: October 1957

Ethnicity: Han Chinese

Year of Joining CCP: April 1983

Education: Completed Post-Graduation in Meteorological Communications from Chengdu School of Meteorology.

Current Designation: Vice-Chairman of TAR PPCC, Commissioner and Party Secretary of Nagchu Party Committee since February 2014.

SONAM RINZIN

Year of Birth: September 1959 in Rinbung County of Shigatse (Ch: Xigaze)

Ethnicity: Tibetan

Year of Joining CCP: May 1981

Education: Completed graduation from Central Party School in June 1981

Current Designation: Vice-Chairman of TAR PPCC, Deputy Chairman of TAR United Front Work Department and Secretary General of Tibet Development Fund Assistance Commission.

TSAMCHUNG (f)

Year of Birth: December 1954 in Shigatse

Ethnicity: Tibetan

Year of Joining CCP: February 1976

Education: Graduated from Central Party School

Current Designation: Vice-Chairman of TAR PPCC.

NGAWANG CHOEPHEL

Year of Birth: September 1963 in Bathang County of Karze (Ch: Ganze) in Sichuan Province

Ethnicity: Tibetan

Year of Joining CCP: March 1989

Education: Has a graduation degree in Sports

Previous Designation: Vice-Chairman of TAR Land and Resource Department from 2011-2013.

Current Designation: Vice-Chairman of TAR PPCC and Chairman of TAR Trade and Industry Bureau since 2013.

10TH TAR PEOPLE'S CONGRESS

The TAR People's Congress is the legislative arm of the TAR People's government and elects the Chairman, Vice Chairmen and senior Government officials. It is headed by a Chairman, who is assisted by 12 Vice Chairmen, a Secretary General, 4 Deputy Secretaries General and a 26-member Standing Committee.

PEMA THINLEY (CH: PEMA CHOLING/PADMA CHOLING)

Year of Birth: October, 1952 in Tengchen County (Ch: Dengqen) in Chamdo Prefecture to a farming family.

Nationality: Tibetan

Current Designation: Member of 18th CCP Central Committee and Chairman of TAR People's Congress.

He joined the People's Liberation Army in Qinghai Province at the age of 17 and served in the army for seventeen years. He joined the Communist Party of China in October 1970.

He believes that there is no "issue of Tibet as such" and that the reincarnation of the 14th Dalai Lama would need approval by the Beijing Government. He also claimed that he and the Karmapa Ughen Thinley Dorje are "mates from the same hometown." He has included monks and nuns over the age of 60 into the Chinese social security network. He is reputed to be a "hardliner". He has been described as a stern yet amicable person.

Vice Chairmen of 10th TAR People's Congress

KARMA

Year of birth: November 1954 in Palgong County in Nagchu (Ch: Nagqu)

Ethnicity: Tibetan (*f*)

Year of Joining CCP: January 1976

Education: Holds a Post-graduate Degree. She studied Political systems from the Tibet Nationalities Institute for a year from January 1972- January 1973.

Current Designation: Vice-Chairman as well as standing committee member of the 10th TAR People's Congress and the President of TAR Women's Federation.

ZHOU CHUNLAI

Year of Birth: August 1954 in Huainan County of Jiangsu Province

Ethnicity: Han Chinese

Year of Joining CCP: April 1975

Education: Has a professional degree in Agronomy

Current Designation: Vice-Chairman and Standing Committee Member of TAR People's Congress since January 29, 2013

ZHAO ZHENXIU

Year of Birth: December 1955 in Cangxi County of Sichuan Province

Ethnicity: Han Chinese

Year of Joining CCP: June 1975

Education: Graduated from Central Party School in December 1970. He worked as squad leader in PLA troops Unit number 81529 from January 1970-1977.

Current Designation: Vice-Chairman and Standing Committee Member of 10th TAR People's Congress.

DORJEE PHAKMO DEKYI CHODON

Year of Birth: December 1942 in Lhasa

Ethnicity: Tibetan (*f*)

Year of Joining CCP: May 1955

Education: Studied till Junior High School and studied Buddhist Scriptures in Samding Monastery after she was recognized as the 12th reincarnation of Dorjee Phakmo of the same monastery.

Current Designation: Vice-Chairman of 10th TAR People's Congress and Standing Committee member of 12th National CPPCC of 18th CCP since March 2013.

SHINGTSA TENZIN CHOEDAK

Year of Birth: October 1950 in Tsomai County of Lhoka (Ch: Shannan)

Ethnicity: Tibetan

Year of Joining CCP: June 1983

Education: Holds graduation degree. He was recognized as a Tulku in Shingza Monastery of Lhoka.

Current Designation: Vice-Chairman of 10th TAR People's Congress since January 2008.

MA JU-LUNG

Year of Birth: August 1952 in Tsongyon County of Amdo (Haiyan of Qinghai Province.

Ethnicity: Muslim

Year of Joining CCP: April 1972

Education: Graduated from Central Party School in February 1969 He worked as squad leader and deputy leader in PLA troops Unit number 8018 from February 1969-February 1974.

Current Designation: Vice-Chairman of 10th TAR People's Congress since January 2008.

DORJEE

Year of Birth: December 1952 in Gyatsa County of Lhoka

Ethnicity: Tibetan

Year of Joining CCP: January 1996

Education: Holds a graduation degree

Current Designation: Vice-Chairman of 10th TAR People's Congress and the Director of China Academy of Engineering.

WU JINHUI

Year of Birth: March 1953 in Cangzhou County of Hebei Province

Ethnicity: Han Chinese

Year of Joining CCP: October 1973

Education: Graduated from Central Party School

Current Designation: Vice-Chairman of 10th TAR People's Congress since January 2011.

ZHAO HEI

Year of Birth: May 1955 in Qu County of Sichuan Province

Ethnicity: Han Chinese

Year of Joining CCP: January 1979

Education: Holds a graduation degree

Current Designation: He was elected as one of the Vice-Chairman of 10th TAR People's Congress on January 29, 2013.

TENZIN NAMGYAL

Year of Birth: July 1959 in Dromo County of Shigatse (Ch: Yadong County of Xigaze)

Ethnicity: Tibetan

Year of Joining CCP: July 1981

Education: Graduated from Central Party School

Current Designation: Vice-Chairman of 10th TAR People's Congress and Party Secretary of Shigatse Prefectural Committee of CCP.

WOESER

Year of Birth: December 1960 in Lhasa.

Ethnicity: Tibetan

Year of Joining CCP: September 1987

Education: Completed graduation in Engineering on July 1985 from Department of Mechanical Engineering of Chongqing University.

Current Designation: Vice-Chairman of 10th TAR People's Congress and Director of TAR Supervision Committee.

LI DAKE (LE DAKE)

Year of Birth: March 1960 in Dongxiang County of Jiangxi Province

Ethnicity: Han Chinese

Year of Joining CCP: March 1983

Education: Completed his PhD in Internantional Relations in December 1976.

Current Designation: Vice-Chairman of 10th TAR People's Congress since January 2013.

The official pin-yin Romanised name is LE Dake. The surname is not too common and the Chinese character "Le" means "happiness."

Le Dake (PhD) received a doctorate in International Relations from the China Institutes of Contemporary International Relations (CICIR), which is affiliated to the Ministry of State Security (MoSS) in Beijing. He is 56 years old and has been in Tibet for 12 years. The first 13 years of his career were spent in the Jiangxi Provincial Public Security Department (he is from Jiangxi Province) where he rose to the rank of a Deputy Head (not to be confused with a Deputy Party Secretary). In 2004 he was appointed Party Secretary and Head of the TAR State Security Department in Lhasa. Since then he has been the top man in Tibet in charge of Counter-Intelligence against India, USA and elsewhere and is also responsible for collecting intelligence on the exile Tibetan communities in India and Nepal.

He vacated this State Security position almost two years ago in January 2013,when he was elevated to the Standing Committee of the TAR People's Congress. The People's Congress is mainly concerned with making and interpreting laws as well as overseeing the TAR judicial and procuratorial system. Le Dake probably is the People's Congress Standing Committee's expert on security issues. He is ranked #14th, which currently is the lowest rank of those on the TAR People's Congress Standing Committee.

In June 2015, Le Dake, became the first leader at the regional level to be detained in Tibet for alleged corruption in the nationwide crackdown on graft. It is unclear whether the investigation was related to his work as Tibet's spy chief or his time in Jiangxi, where corruption was uncovered on a massive scale. The province's former party chief, Su Rong, has also been detained.

Administrative Distribution of TAR by China

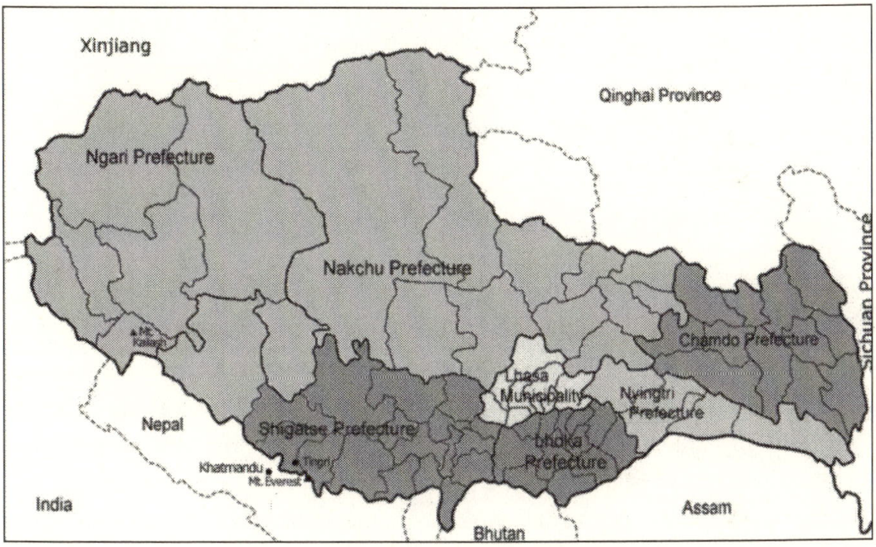

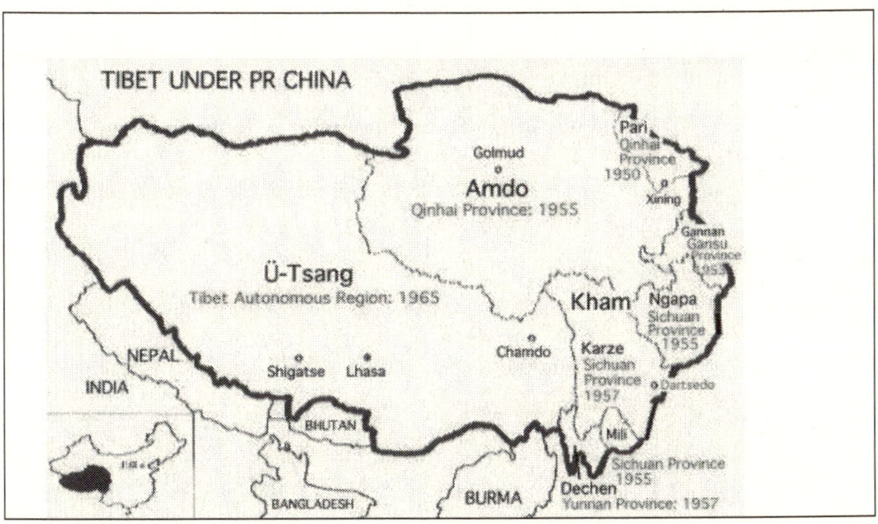

The Tibet Autonomous Region is divided into three (3) Municipalities (shi) and four (4) Prefectures (di-qu).

The three TAR Municipalities are Lhasa, Shigatse and Chamdo. Shigatse was given municipality status in July, 2014, and Chamdo received the same status October 10, 2014. Municipalities are ranked at the same level as prefectures but given a slightly heavier weight and importance. The three TAR municipalities each have a District (qu) which essentially covers the city area that carries their municipality's name and is made up of urban Neighbourhoods (jie-dao) and surrounding Rural Townships (xiang) with their Villages (cun). A District exists at the same administrative level as a county but enjoys a slightly more elevated rank in the administrative hierarchy.

Lhasa Municipality's urban district is named **Cheng-guan District**

Shigatse Municipality's urban district is named **Sang-zhu-zi District**

Chamdo Municipality has renamed the whole Chamdo County as **Ka-ruo District** with 3 urban townships (one of which encompasses the former Chamdo city area and is named **Cheng-guan urban township** because its population is not yet large enough to be considered an urban district) plus 12 rural townships. The name "Ka-ruo" comes from the name of the Stone Age archeological site on the southern outskirts of what now is known as Cheng-guan urban township.

Each of the three Municipalities also includes Counties (xian) with Urban Townships (zhen) and Rural Townships (xiang) with villages.

The four remaining TAR Prefectures are: Lhoka, Nagchu, Ngari and Nyingtri. Each is made up of counties that consist of urban townships and scattered villages under numerous rural townships.

Level #1: The Autonomous Region
Level #2: Municipalities and Prefectures
Level #3: Districts (within a Municipality) and counties
Level #4: Neighbourhoods, Urban and Rural Townships
Level #5: Villages

1., 2., 3., etc = Rank and hierarchy are the essence of any Chinese system or organization. These Lhasa Municipality officials therefore are listed in their official rank order.

NOTE

- This listing is accurate as of 2017.
- There is not one holdover from the Party Standing Committee that existed in late 2012. At this level – one level below the officials at the Autonomous Region level – turnover is much more frequent with several additions and/or subtractions per year.
- Six of the top 7 Municipality Party positions currently are held by non-Han Chinese officials.
- Five Party Standing Committee members are also senior members of the Government, and 4 of these 5 are Aid Tibet cadres.
- Many officials, both Tibetan and Han, reach the top with backgrounds that include security related positions. In this regard, Tibetans are heavily represented top-to-bottom at all levels of the Public Security Bureau and the People's Armed Police. This is a fact that is perhaps not sufficiently well known in the overseas Tibetan community and little known in the international community.
- Aid Tibet cadres from inland China have fundamentally changed the face of TAR officialdom. Lhasa Municipality is mainly aided by Beijing, Jiangsu Province and ministries of the Central Government.
- There are plenty of examples in these two lists that show that a Han Chinese name does not necessarily guarantee that the individual is a Han Chinese.

LHASA MUNICIPALITY

Lhasa Municipality Party Standing Committee

CHOEDAK/CHEDAK

Party Secretary, member of the TAR Party Standing Committee

Ethnicity: Tibetan

Choedak is currently also Chairman of the TAR's United Front Work Department and Party Secretary of Lhasa Municipality.

Choedak is a 58 year old Tibetan from Gyalthang (Zhongdian, Yunnan Province). In 1979 he started his career as a Communist Youth League (CYL) worker which led to an educational administration position as head of the Gyalthang Party School. This was followed by a number of years in propaganda assignments. He was appointed Party Secretary of Gyalthang County in 1994, chief government administrator of Dechen Tibetan Prefecture in 2001 (the year Zhongdian County changed its name to 'Shangri-la' County) and finally Party Secretary of Dechen in 2007. In 2010 he was elevated to the Yunnan Province Communist Party Standing Committee and, shortly thereafter, was transferred to Tibet where he was given a slot on the Tibet Autonomous Region (TAR) Party Standing Committee and initially took responsibility for the TAR United Front Department portfolio. In late 2011 CHOEDAK was appointed Lhasa Party Secretary replacing the Han Chinese Qin Yizhi (who had left Tibet to head the China Youth League from its headquarters in Beijing). As Lhasa Party Secretary, Choedak is the most powerful official in Lhasa municipal politics which covers the city and seven surrounding counties. He represents this large area on the TAR Party Standing Committee where he ranks 8th as an ordinary member.

LOBSANG TENPA

Deputy Party Secretary, Chairman of the Lhasa People's Congress.

Ethnicity: Tibetan

Lobsang Tenpa is a 62 year old Tibetan from Tsome County in Lhoka Prefecture (Shannan). As a teenager during the Cultural Revolution he worked as a paramedic (or what was called a "bare-foot doctor") in the Tsome countryside. Later in 1973 he was sent to Hunan Province to pursue studies in public health, but his career took a change of direction in 1976 with an appointment to the Lhoka Public Security Bureau and a period of study at the China Criminal Police College in Shenyang Liaoning Province. He then gradually rose to eventually head the Lhoka Public Security Bureau while simultaneously working as a Deputy Party Secretary of the Lhoka Political and Legal Committee. In 2002 he moved up a level to the TAR Political and Legal Committee eventually becoming one of its Deputy Party Secretaries. Since the end of 2009 **Lobsang Tenpa** has been a Deputy Party Secretary of the Lhasa Party Standing Committee and Chairman of the Lhasa Municipality People's Congress.

ZHANG YANQING

Born December 1955 in Shanghai. Joined the CCP in January 1971 and began his political career as the deputy head of the Communist Youth League organization in Qinghai province.

Ethnicity: Tibetan

Zhang Yanqing is a 52 -year old Tibetan from Pari County (Tianzhu Tibetan Autonomous County) in Gansu Province. His entire career has been closely connected with policing and security work. Following 14 years in Gansu Province, he was transferred to Lhasa in 1995. Over the subsequent 14 years he held increasingly senior positions in the Lhasa Public Security Bureau. In 2009 he became a Deputy Mayor of Lhasa while still occupying the top spot in the city's Public Security Bureau. In 2012 he joined the Lhasa Party Standing Committee as an ordinary member and also was made Party Secretary of both the Lhasa Political and

Legal Committee and the Lhasa Public Security Bureau. In March 2013 he became a Deputy Party Secretary of the Lhasa Standing Committee and Mayor of Lhasa while retaining the title of Party Secretary in the Lhasa Political and Legal Committee.

CHEN YONG

Born in November 1964, in Qidong, Jiangsu Province.

Is currently **Deputy Party Secretary**, Executive Deputy Mayor of Lhasa Municipality, Party Secretary of the Jiangsu Aid-Tibet Corps (which co-assists Lhasa Municipality)

Ethnicity: Han Chinese

Chen Yong is a 52 -year old Han Chinese from the Nantong area in Jiangsu Province near Shanghai. He studied agricultural economics at Nanjing Agricultural University and then spent the subsequent 26 years of his career alternating between economic development roles and political administrative roles all in the city of Nanjing. For some time he was in charge of Nanjing's water conservancy programs as well as the steady growth of the city's industrial development zone. In 2011 he became Party Secretary of the main Nanjing commercial district.

Only one year later in the summer of 2012, Chen Yong made the decision to join the Jiangsu Province Aid-Tibet Corps and was named its Party Secretary (Aid-Tibet cadre stints normally last 3 years but can be renewed). Upon arrival in Lhasa – which partners with Jiangsu Province and Beijing – he was appointed a Deputy Party Secretary of the Lhasa Party Standing Committee and Executive Vice Mayor of the city. He oversees, and is accountable for, the development projects undertaken in Lhasa by Jiangsu Province. Chen's experience in urban development and technological development is frequently on show in the media. Additionally he is a strong, talented administrator. While in Lhasa, in 2013, he was promoted in absentia to a Deputy Party Secretary position in Nanjing.

He has returned to Nanjing in 2015 as Vice Mayor in charge of assistance to Tibet. (See additional comments on Chen in the Lhasa Government section).

LONG ZHIGANG

Executive Deputy Party Secretary

Ethnicity: Tibetan

Not too much is known about Lhasa's Executive Deputy Secretary (February, 2014). Long Zhigang is Tibetan but from where, so far, remains a mystery.

About a decade ago he was the Party Secretary of Gonjo County in Chamdo Prefecture. He next became a member of the Chamdo Party Standing Committee as well as Party Secretary of the Chamdo Political and Legal Committee and Party Secretary of the Chamdo Public Security Bureau. He then appeared in Lhasa as Deputy Head of the TAR Bureau of Press Information and Publications. By 2012 he was a member of the Lhasa Party Standing Committee and head of the Party's Organization Department in Lhasa. In February 2014, he became the Executive Deputy Secretary of the Lhasa Party Standing Committee.

He also appears to be a strong administrator whom the Party has earmarked for increasingly important postings.

MA XINMING

Born December 1972, in Yi, Lijiang, Yunnan. Joined the CCP in June 1994 and began work in July 1995.

Deputy Party Secretary, Head of the Beijing Aid-Tibet Corps (which co-assists the Lhasa Municipality)

Ethnicity: Han Chinese

Despite possessing a surname usually reserved for the Hui, or Chinese Moslems, Ma Xinming is a 44- year old Yi nationality cadre. His career however has been largely Beijing-based where he graduated from the China University of Political Science and Law and earned a PhD in public administration at Beijing University. From 1995 to 2006 Ma Xinming worked continuously in the Beijing Municipal Bureau of Press Information and Publications which among other things is responsible for all copyright issues in the capital. In 2006 he was transferred to the Beijing Propaganda Department where he handled internal dissemination of Party programs, union activities and grass roots information campaigns in the city.

In 2010 he was named one of the Deputy Heads of that year's Beijing Aid-Tibet Corps cadres which led to an immediate appointment as a Lhasa Vice Mayor. By 2012 he had added membership on the Lhasa Standing Committee to his resume as well as head of the Lhasa Propaganda Department. In 2013 he extended his Aid-Tibet Corps contract for another three years becoming the Corps' head in Lhasa. This decision was rewarded with promotion to Deputy Party Secretary Rank on the Lhasa Standing Committee. He looks after and coordinates all the Beijing-sponsored development projects in Lhasa and its seven counties and is the most publicly visible of the Lhasa Standing Committee members.

DAWA

Deputy Party Secretary, Head of the Lhasa United Front Department, Executive Deputy Leader of the Lhasa Municipality Religious Education Work Leading Small Group.

Ethnicity: Tibetan

Dawa is a 57 year old Tibetan from Nyemo County under Lhasa Municipality. At the start of his career, he spent almost a decade as a primary school teacher in Nyemo. Upon joining the Communist Party in 1984 he attended Lhasa Teacher's College after which he was appointed Vice Principal of Nyemo Middle School and then was shifted to the Nyemo County Government in an education role. In 1991 Dawa was transferred to Lhasa where he spent several years working for the Lhasa Women's Federation. This led to a position in the Lhasa Party's Organization Department initially handling retired cadre issues. By 1996 he was a Deputy Party Secretary of the Lhasa Organization Department, and in 2003 while still a Deputy Party Secretary he also became Director of the Lhasa Commission for Public Sector Reform. Following a couple of refresher courses at the Central Party School in Beijing, he became Head of the Lhasa Party United Front Work Department and a Deputy Chairman of the Lhasa

CPPCC in 2008. In 2010 he was elevated to membership on the Lhasa Party Standing Committee while still retaining the UFWD portfolio. Finally in 2013 he became a Deputy Party Secretary of the Lhasa Standing Committee again without relinquishing his UFWD hat. Normally the head of a UFWD body also holds a senior position on the CPPCC (where in theory many of his non-Party constituents are located) but there are no indications in the Chinese press that Dawa has held a leadership post in the Lhasa CPPCC since 2010. This is unusual.

ZHANG CAIGANG

PLA Commander of the Lhasa Garrison;

Member, Lhasa Party Standing Committee

Ethnicity: Han Chinese

The PLA Commander of the Lhasa Garrison Command is an ex officio member of the Lhasa Party Standing Committee. Such a military appointment normally lasts 2-3 years. He will always occupy the highest ranked ordinary member position (in this case #8) in the Standing Committee. Zhang holds the military rank of Senior Colonel. In China very limited biographical information is ever made available for military and security officials until they reach very senior positions. However prior to being promoted to the Lhasa Garrison position, it is known that he was PLA Commander of the TAR Nagchu Military District. At present the Political Commissar of the Lhasa Garrison Command is Sr. Colonel Xiao Guangfu.

SONAM NYIMA

Member: an Executive Deputy Mayor of Lhasa Municipality.

Ethnicity: Tibetan

Sonam Nyima is a 48 year old Tibetan whose family traces its roots back to Nangchen (Yushu Prefecture, Qinghai Province). At the age of 15 he attended the Tibet School of Finance – a professional/vocational school, which most likely meant his family may then have been living in Lhasa and he probably had a certain level of Chinese language proficiency. His career began in 1982, at the age of 18, in Chamdo County, initially in finance, trade and commerce- related jobs and then, after joining the Communist Party in 1986, in political administrative jobs. Upon reaching the prefecture level in Chamdo, his responsibilities shifted focus to housing and urban-rural development planning before becoming a Chamdo Prefecture Deputy Government Administrator in 2009. In 2011, Sonam Nyima moved up to the regional level as a Deputy Secretary General of the TAR Government. He transferred to the Lhasa Standing Committee and Lhasa Government in mid-2012. (See additional comments on Sonam Nyima in the Lhasa Government section.)

YUAN XUNWANG

Member: Secretary General as well as Party Secretary* for all other miscellaneous organizations that fall under the Lhasa Municipality Party's authority, Director of the Secrets Protection Committee.

Ethnicity: Han Chinese

Very little is known about **Yuan Xunwang**, but he must have been chosen because he represents a safe, reliable pair of hands well experienced in the ways of Lhasa and the TAR. He is both a full member of the Lhasa Party Standing Committee (ranked surprisingly high at #10) and its Secretary General. Often a Secretary General does not enjoy both positions, so this hints that Yuan Xunwang must enjoy considerable seniority and the trust of the TAR Party. As Secretary General he assists, advises, manages the agenda and accompanies Choedak, the Lhasa Party Secretary everywhere. The scant publicly available information on Yuan Xunwang points to a background in Party Discipline Inspection matters. His previous position was with the TAR Discipline Inspection Commission as Director of its Trial Case Office in early 2012. He joined the Lhasa Party Standing Committee in July 2012, six months after Choedak was named Lhasa Party Secretary.

(* This is a position normally shouldered by the Secretary General of a Standing Committee. A notable exception is the TAR Standing Committee where DOTO was given the assignment after his appointment as Party Secretary in Nagchu which, for whatever reasons, went badly and he had to be withdrawn.)

WANG HUI

Member: an Executive Deputy Mayor of Lhasa Municipality , Deputy Party Secretary & Deputy Head of the Jiangsu Aid-Tibet Corps (which co-assists the Lhasa Municipality).

Ethnicity: Han Chinese

Wang Hui is a 46 year old, academically-inclined Han Chinese from Xuzhou in Jiangsu Province. He started his career as a journalist for the Nanjing Daily and the Jingling Evening News primarily writing about economic issues. He then changed careers as a result of an appointment to the Economic Structural Reform Commission of Jiangsu Province where he served for five years while earning a PhD at Nanjing University and spending a post-doctoral year at the University of Toronto in Canada. After returning to Nanjing he was named Director of the Jiangsu Urban Development Research Centre. Two years later in 2006 he was named Director of the Village and Small Town Office in Jiangsu Province's Housing and Urban-Rural Development Department. In 2009 he joined the Jiangsu Aid Tibet Corps as one of its Deputy Heads and was assigned the position of Lhasa Vice Mayor. The job challenge was such that he decided to sign on for a second contract in 2012. In a move similar to his colleague Ma Xinming, he was rewarded with promotion to the Lhasa Standing Committee. (See additional comments on Wang Hui in the Lhasa Municipal Government section.)

TSERING WANGDU

Member, First Deputy Party Secretary of the Lhasa Political and Legal Committee, Party Secretary of the Lhasa Public Security Bureau, Deputy Director of the Lhasa Municipality Comprehensive Management Committee for the Safety of Society, and (at the regional TAR level) Deputy Head of the TAR Public Security Department.

Ethnicity: Tibetan

Consistent with those officials who emerge out of a security background, little information is available for **Tsering Wangdu**. He is obviously a Tibetan but his age, birthplace, Party seniority and complete job history have not yet been released. Prior to reaching the Lhasa Standing Committee, Tsering was the Lhasa Procuratorate General (chief investigative prosecutor) and Party Secretary of the Lhasa Procuratorate. This was followed by his being named Head and Deputy Party Secretary of the Lhasa Public Security Bureau as well as a Deputy Mayor of Lhasa. In June 2013 he was elevated to the Lhasa Standing Committee as a member and made Party Secretary of the Lhasa Public Security Bureau.

In a strictly formal sense Tsering Wangdu is Lhasa's number one law and order official, although informally he probably is out-ranked by the Standing Committee Deputy Party Secretary/ Lhasa Mayor Zhang Yanqing who previously held all these same positions. (Also see CHEN Wenqiang, the new Tibetan Deputy Mayor on the Government side, who replaced Tsering Wangdu in that body.)

CHEN JUN

Member and Head of the Lhasa Organization Department.

Ethnicity: Han Chinese

Chen Jun is a 47 -year old Han Chinese whose ancestral home is in central Henan Province. Coinciding exactly with the Lhasa Monlam revolt of March, 1988, a 19-year old Chen began a 6-month course at the Tibet School of Finance in Lhasa and then quickly was dispatched to Ngari in the far west of the TAR. Such an educational beginning and remote posting seems implausible for someone from distant Henan unless, as suspected, Chen Jun, is a second generation Han Chinese cadre who grew up in Tibet and possesses some Tibetan language skills. Handling largely office administrative jobs, he spent 4 years in Gertse County and 4 years in Gar County (Gartok) before being elevated to Ngari Prefecture level administration duties that included secretarial work. Chen's first shift in career direction came in 2000 when he was sent back down to the county level in Ngari but this time as a member of the Gergye County Party Standing Committee and head of its Organization Department. Following over two years in Gergye County, a total of almost 15 years in Ngari and some distance adult education courses from the Beijing Electronic Science and Technology Institute, Chen was transferred at the beginning of 2003 to the TAR level in Lhasa where he entered the Administrative Office of the Party's Organization Department. By mid-2007 he had become Director of the TAR Organization Department's Administrative Office. His next stop at the beginning of 2012 was Lhoka Prefecture where he was named a member of the Party Standing Committee and head of the prefecture's Organization Department. In February 2014 Chen was back in Lhasa appointed a member of the Lhasa Municipal Standing Committee and head of the Lhasa Organization Department. His background is strong on administration and staffing, but his formal education level is light compared to his other Party colleagues.

HONG JIAZHI

Member and Executive Deputy Mayor of Lhasa Municipality and Deputy Head of the Beijing Aid-Tibet Corps.

Ethnicity: Tiajia

Hong Jiazhi is a 42 -year old Tujia nationality cadre from Hubei Province. He attended the Beijing University of Science and Technology (1992-1996) where he became a Communist Party member and obtained a BS degree in Industrial Engineering followed later by a MS in Industrial Management. Over the course of the next 16 years he remained within the university community rising gradually in responsibility as he helped with the incubation and development of four different companies attached to the university and staffed by some of its best graduates and faculty. Eventually he became Deputy General Manager of one of these companies, the Science & Technology Park Co. Ltd and Director of its Management Committee Office while at the same time acting as General Manager and Deputy Party Secretary of another, the Science & Technology Enterprise Group. In mid-2012 Hong was handed something completely new— a political position as a Deputy Government Head of the largely rural district of Beijing named Mentougou (门头沟), which is a hilly agricultural area lying to the far west of the capital at the extreme end of the Western Hills. Its population was then about 290,000 (similar to that of Cheng-guan, the urban area of Lhasa). A year later in August 2013 he was appointed Deputy Head of the latest Beijing Aid Tibet Corps group and appointed as a Lhasa Deputy Mayor. In December, after only several months in Lhasa, his rank was given a boost to Executive Deputy Mayor and membership on the Lhasa Party Standing Committee. (See additional comments on Hong in the Lhasa Municipality Government section.)

ZHOU PUGUO

Member, and a Deputy Mayor of Lhasa Municipality

Ethnicity: Han Chinese

Personal information on **Zhou Puguo** is scarce but he appears to be a Han Chinese who was sent to Tibet in May, 2013 by the Ministry of Agriculture in Beijing as the Ministry's contribution to the Aid Tibet program. Over the last year he has travelled extensively among the seven counties and one district under Lhasa's jurisdiction examining the agricultural production of each and stressing everywhere the need to meet all food quality standards for the sake of consumer safety. (See additional comments on Zhou Puguo in the Lhasa Municipality Government section).

GUO GUO

Member, and Party Secretary of Cheng-guan District (urban and suburban rural Lhasa).

Ethnicity: Tibetan

Guo Guo is a 48 year old Tibetan from Maldrogongkar County whose career began as a 16 year old civilian secretary/assistant in Zha-xue, a Maldrogongkar rural township. This led to a series of jobs in the county Communist Party Organization Department culminating in 1993 when he was named a Deputy Party Secretary of the Maldrogongkar Organization Department.

In 1995 at the age of 27, he was reassigned to Lhasa as a Deputy Party Secretary in the Lhasa branch of the Communist Youth League. Guo Guo's next stop was seven-plus years in the Lhasa Cultural Affairs Bureau followed by a couple of years in the Lhasa Tourism Bureau. In both of these two postings he was a Deputy Party Secretary. In 2007 he was sent down to Nyemo County as Deputy Party Secretary and County Head of Government.

Three years later he was promoted to Deputy Mayor of Lhasa, and in August of 2013, Guo Guo became a member of the Lhasa Party Standing Committee while simultaneously holding the position of Party Secretary for the important Cheng-guan District which encompasses the entire urban and suburban area of Lhasa.

DAMDUL

Member and Head of the Lhasa Propaganda Department.

Ethnicity: Tibetan

"Damdul" is a very common name in Tibet shared by many officials. It is most likely this "Damdul" is the one who during the 2010-to-2011 period was a member of the TAR Discipline Inspection Committee. All that is known for certain is that Damdul, a Tibetan, was appointed Deputy Mayor of Lhasa in July 2012. In this capacity he looked after Lhasa Radio and TV broadcasting, the Lhasa Culture Bureau, Lhasa Tourism and was the Government liaison with the Lhasa Youth League and the Lhasa Culture & Arts Association. One of his last assignments as

Vice Mayor was to make an overseas tour of North America (the USA and Canada) in January, 2014. His interviews on this tour make it obvious that Damdul is articulate and well-educated. When he returned to Lhasa in February, he was promoted to the Lhasa Party Standing Committee and was made Head of its Propaganda Department, a post previously held by his colleague Ma Xinming.

PENG TAO

Member and Lhasa Party Secretary for Discipline Inspection

Ethnicity: Han Chinese

Peng Tao is the most recent addition to the Lhasa Party Standing Committee and so far remains an enigma. He joined the Standing Committee in August, 2014. Any official chosen for the Party discipline role on a Standing Committee usually possesses at least some similar previous experience with a strong, unblemished record. So far Peng Tao's record has not been made public which, as mentioned above, is consistent with officials in military, security and Party discipline fields.

Research is made difficult by Peng Tao's name which is extremely common in China (its holder can be male or female, Han or even Tibetan). Some commentators have suggested that he is Peng Yitao (彭祎涛) who currently is the Party Secretary of Chushur County west of Lhasa – and the photographic likeness is very similar – but why would he change his name by dropping the middle character? It would be a very un-Chinese thing to do. We must therefore await the release of Peng's biography .

YUAN XUNWANG

Secretary General, as well as full Standing Committee Member

Ethnicity: Han Chinese

ZHANG HUI

Executive Deputy Secretary General

Ethnicity: Han Chinese

Previously **Zhang Hui** was a Deputy Secretary General to the Lhasa Municipal Government after which he moved to the Lhasa Cultural Relics Bureau eventually becoming its head (but not its Party Secretary). Moving back to work as Secretary General for the Party's Standing Committee in Lhasa represents a further step up the promotion ladder.

Note: There are another 12-15 ordinary Deputy Secretary Generals who assist individual members of the Standing Committee and/or handle specialist topics for the Standing Committee.

Lhasa Municipal Government

ZHANG YANQING

He is Mayor of Lhasa Municipality, Lhasa Municipality Party Standing Committee Deputy Secretary, Lhasa Municipality Political and Legal Committee Party Secretary, Director of the Lhasa Municipality Comprehensive Management Committee for the Safety of Society, Director of the Lhasa Municipality Emergency Management Committee.

Ethnicity: Tibetan

Zhang Yanqing is an Amdo Tibetan public security specialist who has spent almost 20 years in the TAR. He replaced Dorjee Tsedup as Mayor in early 2013 and holds the #3 Lhasa Municipality Party position as well. Assisted by Jiang Hua, the Government Secretary General, he has overall responsibility for the smooth functioning of well over a 100 Lhasa Municipal Government departments, bureaux, offices, committees and small groups. Zhang liaises directly with the Municipality People's Congress and, in light of his own expertise, with the Lhasa Garrison Command. (See additional comments on Zhang Yanqing in the Lhasa Municipality Party section)

CHEN YONG

Executive Deputy Mayor of Lhasa Municipality, Deputy Secretary of the Lhasa Municipality Party Standing Committee, Party Secretary of the Jiangsu Aid Tibet Corps.

Ethnicity: Han Chinese

Chen Yong is a seasoned Han Chinese who brought considerable Nanjing urban administrative experience to Lhasa when he arrived in August 2012. He is responsible for the municipality's overall economic health monitoring the Finance Bureau, the

Development & Reform Committee, municipality grain supply, municipality price stability, the State Tax Bureau and the Statistics Bureau. He also is responsible for all liaison with the Lhasa Municipality CPPCC. (See additional comments on Chen in the Lhasa Municipality Party section)

SONAM NYIMA

He is Executive Deputy Mayor of Lhasa Municipality, Member of the Lhasa Municipality Party Standing Committee.

Ethnicity: Tibetan

Sonam Nyima is a Khampa Tibetan from Yushu Prefecture in Qinghai whose early work experience was gained almost exclusively in Chamdo and focused heavily on urban-rural planning and development. As Executive Deputy Mayor, Sonam Nyima is charged with oversight of all ethnic and religious work through the Lhasa municipality's Ethnic & Religious Affairs Bureau, of which he seemingly had little past experience. Additionally he oversees the Commission for Municipality Administration and the Environment, the Forestry & Landscape Bureau, the municipality's post office, the Lhasa Electricity Supply Company, the Lhasa Gas Heating Company, the Potala Square Management Committee, the Lhasa Cultural Relics Bureau. He is also involved in determining the suitability of projects proposed for the old, historical district of Lhasa around the Bharkor. Last, but not least, he is the official municipality liaison with the Lhasa branch of the Buddhist Association of China. (See additional comments on Sonam Nyima in the Lhasa Municipality Party section)

WANG HUI

He is Executive Deputy Mayor of Lhasa Municipality, Member of Lhasa Municipality Party Standing Committee , Deputy Party Secretary & Deputy Head of the Jiangsu Aid Tibet Corps (based in Lhasa Municipality).

Ethnicity: Han Chinese

Wang Hui is a Han Chinese urban-rural development specialist with rich experience in the Nanjing region. Mid-career he joined the Jiangsu Aid Tibet Corps and was named its Deputy Head arriving in Lhasa Municipality in September 2009 as a Deputy Mayor. In 2012 he renewed his 3 year commitment to Tibet and was rewarded with a promotion to Executive Deputy Mayor and membership on the Lhasa Municipality Party Standing Committee. His Executive Deputy Mayor duties include supervision of the Lhasa Urban Planning Land & Resources Bureau, the Urban-Rural Planning Bureau, the Housing & Urban-Rural Construction Bureau, the Aid Tibet Lhasa Municipality Office (overseeing and vetting pre-project feasibility studies), and two state enterprises, i.e., the Lhasa Construction Investment Management Co, Ltd. and the Landmark Investment Development Co. Ltd. Wang Hui also exercises direct responsibility for all Jiangsu Province projects in Lhasa Municipality's one district and seven counties. (See additional comments on Wang Hui in the Lhasa Municipal Party section.)

HONG JIAZHI

He is Executive Deputy Mayor of Lhasa Municipality, Member of the Lhasa Municipality Party Standing Committee, and Deputy Head of the Beijing Aid Tibet Corps (based in Lhasa Municipality).

Ethnicity: Tujia

Hong Jiazhi is a Tujia nationality cadre from Hubei Province who has spent the two previous decades in Beijing. His present municipal government responsibilities seem to center on the highly sensitive issue of employment in Lhasa with oversight of the Bureau of Human Resources & Social Security, the Lhasa School of Public Administration, the Lhasa Employment Bureau, the Office of the "Four Work Projects" (programs to improve employability of workers), as well as developmental projects in Lhasa financed by Beijing Municipality. (See additional comments on Hong Jiazhi in the Lhasa Municipality Party section).

ZHOU PUGUO

He is Deputy Mayor, Member of the Lhasa Municipality Party Standing Committee.

Ethnicity: Han Chinese

While there are more articles on the Chinese internet mentioning **Zhou Puguo** than almost any other Deputy Mayor, yet surprisingly there is little personal information about him like age, ethnicity, place of birth, education, Party membership etc. All that is known is that for the decade preceding his transfer to Lhasa in the summer of 2013, he was a highly visible, middle ranking Ministry of Agriculture official in Beijing who was a popular speaker on agricultural issues at conferences, research institutes and local government gatherings all over the country. He has lectured the width and breath of China on such diverse topics as grain production, edible oil producing crops, tea cultivation, traditional medicine attributes, vegetable cultivation mixes according to geography, the importance of edible mushrooms etc. The earliest references noticed describe Zhou Puguo as a researcher, then Deputy Section Chief and finally Section Chief of the Ministry's Economic Crops Section. This was followed by the position of Deputy Inspector and finally in 2009 Deputy Department Head of the Ministry of Agriculture's Crop Cultivation Management Department.

On arrival in Lhasa, on secondment from the Ministry of Agriculture as part of its contribution to the Aid Tibet program, Zhou Puguo was immediately made a member of the Lhasa Municipality Party Standing Committee and a Lhasa Municipality Deputy Mayor. As Deputy Mayor his duties deal exclusively with agriculture in the larger Lhasa Municipality area, and he oversees the Lhasa Agriculture and Animal Husbandry Bureau, the Lhasa Office of the Leading Small Group on Poverty Alleviation and Development, the Agricultural Comprehensive Development Office and the Lhasa August 1st Farm set up originally by the People's Liberation Army in 1951 to produce vegetables for its soldiers. (See an additional comment on Zhou Puguo in the Lhasa Municipality Party section).

JIGME NAMGYAL

Deputy Mayor

Ethnicity: Tibetan

Jigme Namgyal is a 62 year old Tibetan from Shigatse whose father, Chantung·Ji Jigme aka Che Jigme, was one of 20th century Tibet's more prominent officials. When Jigme Namgyal was only 10 years old, his father was dismissed from office and two years later the Cultural Revolution erupted both guaranteeing him an inauspicious start to his career. In 1970 as a 16 year old 'educated youth,' he was sent to the 'Mada Commune' in nearby Panam County, Shigatse Prefecture where he spent 5 years as a translator (he was fluent in Chinese as was his father) and an 'untrained volunteer' local teacher. In 1976 Jigme Namgyal was transferred to the Panam county town as a regular teacher in the county's only middle school. By 1980 the political verdict against his father had just been posthumously reversed allowing rehabilitation of his family name and opening the way for Jigme Namgyal, at 26, to attend Tibet University in Lhasa. There he majored in Tibetan Language & Literature.

During the course of his university studies, the 10th Panchen Lama 'borrowed' him for two years to act – like his father once had done – as one of his secretaries.

Upon graduation in 1986 he was assigned to the Culture & History Office under the Tibet PPCC and a year or so after this he also became an official translator for the Tibet PPCC. Within a few years he had become the Deputy Director of the Cultural & Historical Materials Office (the above body, renamed) and Director of the Translation Office. Between mid-1998 and 2002 he was the Director of the Proposal (Vetting) Committee of the Tibet PPCC, and in 2003 he became a Deputy Secretary General of the 8th Tibet PPCC.

Since mid-2005 Jigme Namgyal has been a Deputy Mayor of Lhasa. Normally a Deputy Mayor will be a Communist Party member, but it seems that Jigme Namgyal may be the lone exception at the top of the Lhasa Government. While his Deputy Mayor job responsibilities have shifted a bit over the last nine years, Jigme Namgyal continues to oversee the city's Civil Affairs Bureau, its Education Bureau, the Lhasa Teacher Training & Vocational Education School, the Tibetan Language Work Committee Office, the Lhasa Earthquake Bureau and the Lhasa Disabled Persons Federation. It is puzzling in light of his possible non-Party status and his previous long relationship with TAR PPCC that he became a Deputy Mayor on the Government side rather than a Vice Chairman of the Lhasa PPCC. Given his age, Jigme Namgyal will be retiring soon.

Historical Footnote: A few words about **Chantung· Ji Jigme (1910-1978)** may help place his son's career in perspective. In 1926 Ji Jigme and an uncle together left home in Zhethongmon Dzong, Shigatse and travelled to Beijing. There he studied Chinese for several years before joining the administration of the 9th Panchen Lama who then was in exile in China. He quickly rose up the non-religious side of the Panchen Lama's Khenpo Assembly and was rewarded with the Directorship of the 9th Panchen Lama's Representative Office in Chungking, Sichuan. Later as the 9th Panchen Lama's chief private secretary he managed the frustratingly complex efforts to facilitate the 9th Panchen Lama's return to Shigatse and Tashilunpo Monastery. In 1937 when the 9th Panchen Lama died in Jyekundo, Qinghai short of his goal, Ji Jigme was involved in all the behind the scenes political maneuvering to choose the 10th Panchen Lama. Then and later, he seems to have been the main access conduit to the Panchen Lama for the Nationalist (KMT) Government as well as the often more powerful warlords in Qinghai, Gansu and Xikang (Hsikang) provinces.

After WWII, Ji Jigme moved the Panchen Lama's Office to Nanking were he continued cooperation with the KMT and for a short period actually became a KMT legislator representing Tibet in Nanking. In 1948, however, he refused to follow Chiang Kai-shek to Taiwan. He informed Chiang Kai-shek that the young 10th Panchen Lama would remain in Qinghai and then switched allegiance to the Chinese Communist Party. At this point he was equivalent to the 10th Panchen Lama's civilian chief minister and tirelessly argued for the restoration of the Panchen Lama's traditional rights vis-à-vis the Lhasa Government. Ji Jigme brought the 10th Panchen Lama to Beijing in 1951 to meet Mao Zedong and then, thanks to a last minute Chinese intercession, personally participated in the 17 Point Agreement negotiations as the only non-Lhasa Tibetan delegate. When the PLA 18th Army marched into Tibet, Ji Jigme joined General Fan Ming and the Independent Brigade sent by General Peng Dehuai's Northwest Field Army in support of the 18th Army. Elements of the Independent Brigade also picked up the 10th Panchen Lama and escorted him from Qinghai to Lhasa and then to Shigatse. During the 1950s in Tibet there was no more adroit a Tibetan politician than Ji Jigme. A good bit of the tension that existed between Lhasa and Shigatse was due to his considerable political skills and many contacts in Beijing. When the 10th Panchen Lama penned his famous 70,000 character criticism of Chinese policies in Tibet in 1962 and then was removed from all his posts and sent to prison in 1964, Ji Jigme suffered a similar fate. But unlike his holy patron, he disappeared for good from the Tibet political stage.

TSERING YANGZOM *(f)*

Deputy Mayor

Ethnicity: Tibetan

Tsering Yangzom is a 54 year old Tibetan from Chamdo who studied electrical and hydro-electrical engineering at the Tibet Nationality Institute in Shaanxi Province. She began her career as a technician in Gongkar County, Lhoka Prefecture and then spent the next 24 years in Chushur County under Lhasa Municipality in a variety of technical and economic roles eventually becoming the Deputy Head of the Chushur Government administration. In 2002 she was transferred up the Lhasa River to Tagtse County as its Deputy Party Secretary and Head of Government. Finally in 2010 Tsering Yangzom was named a Deputy Mayor of Lhasa. As Vice Mayor her major responsibilities are public health and livelihood issues. She oversees the Water Conservancy Bureau, the Public Health Bureau, the Population & Family Planning

Committee, the Lhasa Food & Drug Administration, the Lhasa People's Hospital, the Weather Bureau, the Lhasa Working Committee on Children & Women, and the Lhasa Safe Living Office. She is also the government liaison person for the Lhasa Women's Association and the Lhasa Science Federation

CHEN WENQIANG

He is Deputy Mayor, Deputy Party Secretary of the TAR Public Security Bureau (PSB), Deputy Party Secretary of the Lhasa Municipality Political & Legal Committee , Head of the Lhasa Municipality Public Security Bureau (PSB) as well as its Deputy Party Secretary, and 1st Political Commissar of the Lhasa People's Armed Police (PAP) branch.

Ethnicity: Han Chinese

Career information on officials with security, military and Party discipline backgrounds is often kept confidential for as long as possible. All that is known about Chen Wenqiang is that prior to his occupying the present set of security posts, he was a Deputy Head of the TAR State Security Bureau (SSB) and head of its Lhasa Municipality branch department which is concerned with counter intelligence gathering and focuses on the overseas Tibetan community as well as all foreign passport holders working and living in the TAR.

The PSB and SSB have a large number of carefully selected and nurtured Tibetan senior officers (e.g., the present Mayor of Lhasa, Zhang Yanqing and Chen Wenqiang's predecessor as Vice Mayor, Tsering Wangdu) and indeed references in news items suggest that Chen Wenqiang is also a Tibetan, possibly from the peripheral regions of Kham or Amdo where it is not uncommon for Tibetans to carry both a Tibetan and a Chinese name. It is no surprise that Chen Wenqiang's role in the present government administration is to deal with the city's security issues. He is the Deputy Mayor who looks after the Lhasa State Security Department, the Municipal Bureau of Letters and (Telephone) Calls, the Lhasa Administration for Work Safety, the Lhasa Foreign Affairs Office, the Urban Comprehensive Law

Enforcement Unit, and the Communications Comprehensive Law Enforcement Unit. He also is the official municipal government liaison with the Lhasa PAP and Lhasa PSB.

SUN XIAONAN

He is Deputy Mayor Deputy Party Secretary and Deputy Head of the Jiangsu Aid Tibet Corps

Ethnicity: Han Chinese

Sun Xiaonan is a 54 year old Han cadre from Jiangsu Province who arrived in Tibet in 2012. He concurrently retains the rank of Deputy Mayor of Zhenjiang City, Jiangsu Province with a population 3.2 million, located on the Yangtze River between Yangzhou and Nanjing and has over 30 years of urban commercial development experience. His primary Government responsibilities include supervising all private sector economic development in Lhasa including the Lhasa Commerce Bureau, the China Merchants Group (oldest company in China, 1872), the Lhasa Industry & Commerce Administrative Management Bureau, the Lhasa Administration of Quality and Technology Supervision plus the Lhasa branches of China Telecom, China Mobile and the China Postal Savings Bank. In addition Sun Xiaonan shoulders his share of supervision responsibility for some of Jiangsu Provinces projects in Lhasa, provides assistance and advice to the Lhasa Development & Reform Commission and is the city's official liaison with the Lhasa Industry & Commerce Federation and the Lhasa branch of the All China Federation of Trade Unions

XU ZONGJUN

He is Deputy Mayor, a Deputy Head of the Beijing Aid Tibet Corps

Ethnicity: Han Chinese

Xu Zongjun is a 51 year old Han Chinese cadre from Beijing who joined the Communist Party in 1986 when he graduated from Zhongshan University (Guangzhou, Guangdong) in History. His political career started in the Fangshan District of

Beijing Municipality where he played a support role in economic planning. On-the-job experience was supplemented by a number of graduate courses in economic management at the Beijing Party School. He soon became Deputy Director of the District's Planning Committee. Success there led to an appointment as a political officer in the smaller Doudian Township on the far southwest fringes of Beijing Municipality. It was then a rather small town of about 54,000 populations and an economy that needed stimulation. Hard work and a little luck in building the economy led to promotions as Deputy Party Secretary, head of Government administration and finally Party Secretary. This record propelled Xu Zongjun back up to the Fangshan District in a much more senior role than he had enjoyed before. In 2009 he became Deputy Party Secretary and Director of the Fangshan Development and Reform Commission.

In late June 2013, Xu Zongjun joined the Beijing Aid Tibet Corps and took up his new post of Deputy Mayor of Lhasa Municipality in August that year. Xu Zongjun's portfolio in Lhasa is one that deals with the city's legal and governance issues. He monitors the Office of the Lhasa Integrated Governance Commission, the Lhasa Justice Bureau, the Municipal People's Government Law Office, the Lhasa Citizens Service Centre and the Lhasa Civil Air Defense Office. He is the municipality's official liaison with the Lhasa Intermediate People's Court and the Lhasa People's Procuratorate.

YANG ANWEN

Deputy Mayor

Ethnicity: Tujia

Yang Anwen is a Tujia nationality cadre from Hubei Province. He attended what appears to be a vocational, two year specialist program in Forestry Management at the West Hubei Forestry School. Yang Anwen , who is in his mid 40s, began his career at the grass roots level in his native Xianfeng County of Enshi Tujia & Miao Nationalites Autonomous Prefecture. He was involved in Party building and Communist Youth League work in Xianfeng villages and rural townships. In 2001 he was promoted out of Xianfeng County and brought to Wuhan to run the administrative and financial affairs offices of Hubei Province's Education Department. Following two years in Wuhan, Yang Anwen was sent back to Enshi Prefecture as a member of the Xuanen County Party Standing Committee and head of the Party's Organization Department. In January 2006, he was selected as a member of a small mid-career cadre group that was sent to the University of Chicago in the USA for a 6-month refresher course in public administration and economics. When he returned to Wuhan, Yang Anwen was promoted to head the Government administration of Hefeng County, also in Enshi Prefecture, with a population of 225,000. In mid 2008, Yang Anwen was again given a short sabbatical leave and sent to Beijing where he served a 6-month temporary assignment as Assistant Director of the Ministry of Finance's Comprehensive Reform Office. Returning to Hefeng County, Yang Anwen became its Party Secretary in October 2011.

Although Hubei Province officially has twinned up with Lhoka Prefecture, not Lhasa Municipality, it still looks like Yang Anwen may have joined the Hubei Aid Tibet Corps in 2013 and was then posted to Lhasa as a Deputy Mayor. In Lhasa his forte seems largely to be in the area of industrial zone development. He is in charge of overseeing the Lhasa Environmental Protection Bureau, the Lhasa Economic and Technology Development Zone Management Committee, the Liuwu New District Management Committee, the Tagtse County Industrial Park, the Chushur County Industrial Park and the Toelung Dechen County Industrial Park. He additionally assists the municipality in all its commercial merchandising efforts.

SHI BENLIN

Deputy Mayor

Ethnicity: Han Chinese

Shi Benlin is a 47 year old Han cadre from Henan Province who graduated from the Henan University of Technology and possesses a PhD in Mining Engineering from the Jiaozuo Institute of Technology that is now in Jiangsu Province. During this period Shi Benlin was Party Secretary of the Communist Youth League branch in each of these educational institutions. His entire pre-Tibet career has been spent in Henan, particularly in Jiaozuo Municipality on the north bank of the Yellow River opposite Zhengzhou the provincial capital where he was Party Secretary of the Commerce Bureau and the Foreign Commercial Investment Services Bureau. More recently Shi Benlin served in Changge Municipality in central Henan, which is a city of 700,000 population, noted among other things for its non-ferrous metal production. After a steady string of promotions, Shi Benlin became Party Secretary of Changge Municipality in August, 2012.

Exactly one year later he was functioning in Lhasa as a Deputy Mayor. At present Henan Province does not have a formal Aid Tibet Corps program, but it seems likely that Shi Benlin was recruited to Lhasa because something in his background – perhaps foreign investment management or state resource management which would include mining -- was deemed useful. If so he would be an Aid Tibet cadre. As Deputy Mayor, Shi Benlin looks after the Lhasa Industry & Information Technology Bureau, the Lhasa State Owned Asset Supervision and Administration Commission, the Lhasa Technology Bureau, all State owned enterprises that operate under the authority of Lhasa Municipality and the Lhasa Finance Office. He assists with the Lhasa Development & Reform Commission and liaises regularly with the Lhasa Science & Technology Federation and all Ministry of Finance officials from Beijing who are working in Lhasa.

WU YASONG

Deputy Mayor

Ethnicity: Han Chinese

Wu Yasong is a 53 year old Han Chinese who was born in Xianyang, Shaanxi Province, a suburban town near Xian where the Tibet Nationality Institute is located. He arrived with his parents in Chamdo in 1968 as a five year old youngster and grew up there. As a result Wu Yasong is totally fluent in Tibetan and is referred to as a "2nd generation Tibet cadre."

He went to university in Chongqing and has a degree in journalism. Wu Yasong's career began in 1985 when he became a reporter for the Tibet Daily newspaper. After a decade or so, he was encouraged to change hats and so became a Deputy Chief of the News Section in the TAR Party's Propaganda Department. Later he became Head of the Propaganda Department's Education Section. In the summer of 2014 Wu was promoted to Deputy Mayor of Lhasa Municipality. He has taken over the portfolio of responsibilities left by Damdul when he moved up to the Lhasa Municipality Party Standing Committee. This means Wu Yasong is heavily involved in tourism and the promotion of Tibetan culture. He oversees the Lhasa Tourism Bureau, the Lhasa Cultural Affairs Bureau, the Lhasa Radio, Film and Television Bureau, the Lhasa News Publication Bureau, the Lhasa Potala Cultural Tourism Company and the proposed Cultural Tourism Park in Tsejiao Ling (in a Lhasa rural township on the south side of the Lhasa River). He is also the government liaison official for the Lhasa Communist Youth League and the Lhasa Federation of Literary & Art Circles.

Historical Footnote: Wu Yasong's family history is inextricably connected with the history of Tibet over the last half century. His father, Wu Jianli, entered Tibet in 1951 with the Northwest Field Army's Independent Brigade. He was the personal secretary of General Fan Ming who commanded the Brigade and escorted the 10th Panchen Lama back to Shigatse. This Brigade – made up of troops from the 1st Army in Lanzhou – then established headquarters in Shigatse and proceeded to influence events and policies from Shigatse all the way to Ngari in the west. General Fan Ming was a contrarian who held strong opinions about Tibetan history. He constantly lobbied Beijing for faster social change in Tibet and urged China's leaders to work with and through the "more patriotic" Panchen Lama rather than the Dalai Lama. He was frequently at loggerheads with the 18th Army which controlled Lhasa and often chose to ignore or water down policy guidelines issued from Beijing. In 1958 General Fan Ming was labeled a 'rightist' and removed from Tibet. As Fan Ming's personal secretary, Wu Jianli was tarred with the same 'rightist' brush. He returned to Xian and despite his 'rightist' label luckily found a job at the Tibet Nationality Institute teaching Tibetan language classes. Wu Jianli was an ardent admirer of Tibetan culture. In 1968 at the height of the Cultural Revolution when chaos prevailed and the Tibet Nationality Institute was effectively closed down, a cry for help arrived from Chamdo where a newly formed Tibetan commune desperately needed a Tibetan speaker with professional accounting skills. Wu Jianli who by this time was married and had a young son saw this as his chance to return. Under normal circumstances a 'rightist' would not be considered, but no one else volunteered to go. So in 1968 Wu Jianli and his family travelled back to the TAR and Dragyab County in Chamdo Prefecture. Having been burned politically in Shigatse a decade earlier and having already experienced the political unpredictability and myriad dangers of the Cultural Revolution, Wu Jianli chose to spend most of his time collecting production data from remote nomad encampments away from other Han Chinese. The fact that his wife who accompanied him everywhere was a medical doctor helped give them the excuse to linger indefinitely in remote villages and nomad areas in order to better "serve the people." As a result their son – now a Deputy Mayor of Lhasa – grew up speaking more Tibetan than Chinese. In an ending dripping with political irony, Wu Jianli was named a "National Model Worker," only the second "rightist" in the history of the Chinese Communist Party to ever accomplish such a feat.

JIANG HUA

Secretary General of the Lhasa Government

Ethnicity: Tibetan

Jiang Hua is another example of a Tibetan with a Chinese sounding name. Except for occasional references which mention that Jiang Hua was previously the Government Head of Maldrogongkar County and for a decade headed the Lhasa Tourism Bureau, little biographical material publicly exists about him. His main job as Government Secretary General has been to assist Zhang Yanqing and, to a lesser extent, Chen Yong, in their daily work. To this end he is in charge of the Municipal Government Office, the Municipal Government Research Office, the Municipal Government Reception Office and the Lhasa Municipal Government branch offices in Beijing and Chengdu. Directly under Jiang Hua are 13 Han and Tibetan Deputy Secretaries General who serve the remainder of the Deputy Mayors.

Lhasa Municipality Cheng-guan District Party Leaders Standing Committee

The Cheng-guan District is composed of the entire Lhasa urban area totaling 8 large neighborhoods plus the surrounding suburban area made up of 4 rural townships each with a number of natural villages. It should not be confused with the higher level of administration termed the "Lhasa Municipality" which is one notch above a district and has a jurisdiction much larger than just the Cheng-guan District. If the word "mayor" refers to the highest official closest to the population of a city, the head of the Cheng-guan District's Government, **LIU Liang,** probably deserves the title of *Lhasa Mayor* rather than **ZHANG Yanqing** who at the Municipality level is in charge of Government matters over seven (7) counties as well as the Cheng-guan District. In the eyes of Lhasa citizens and the Communist Party, however, Cheng-guan District Party Secretary **GUO GUO** is the most powerful and recognizable figure in town.

GUO GUO

He is Party Secretary, Member of the Lhasa Municipality Party Standing Committee.

Ethnicity: Tibetan

Guo Guo's short biography can be found above in the Lhasa Municipality Party Standing Committee listing. (Page 67) (Comment: To speculate about what sort of career path GUO GUO might expect in the future, it may be interesting to note where his Party Secretary predecessors are today. His immediate predecessor, PHURBU DONDUP ***(Pu-bu Dun-zhu)***, was sent to the political hotspot Nagchu Prefecture as a Deputy Party Secretary and head of Nagchu's Organization Department while

PHURBU DONDUP's predecessor, TRINLEY DORJE **(Chilie Duo-ji)**, is now Director of the Ethnic and Religious Affairs Committee of the Tibet Autonomous Region.)

MA YONGQING

He is Deputy Party Secretary, Party Secretary and Chairman of Cheng-guan District People's Congress.

Ethnicity: Muslim

Ma Yongqing is a Lhasa native born into its Kachee (Kashmiri) Moslem community in 1959. At the age of 14 he was sent to the Tibet Nationality Institute in Shaanxi Province to study Tibetan language and literature. He spent six years in this school. He started his career in 1979 doing various office administration tasks for the Cheng-guan Government and then spent two years with the Cheng-guan Youth League. Thereafter what followed was a focus on law and the Chinese legal system. First he was a judicial officer in the Cheng-guan Intermediate Court. After years of service this eventually led to promotion as a Deputy Chief Justice and then Deputy Chief Procurator in the Cheng-guan District. In 2005 Ma Yongqing was transferred to Tagtse County where he spent five years as its Chief Procurator. In 2010 he was named a Deputy Party Secretary of the Cheng-guan Party Standing Committee and both Party Secretary and Chairman of the Cheng-guan People's Congress. Ma Yongqing is possibly the most experienced and knowledgeable of his present Party colleagues concerning Lhasa and its distinctive features.

LIU LIANG

He is Deputy Party Secretary, and Head of Government (as well as Party Secretary within the Government Party cell)

Ethnicity: Han Chinese

Liu Liang, at the age of 41, is the youngest of the leaders of the four pillars (i.e. Party, People's Congress, Government and CPPCC) in Cheng-guan District. It is very likely that he was born in Tibet because he attended the Tibet Agricultural & Animal Husbandry College in Nyingtri Prefecture. After graduation he spent two years working on agricultural and pastoral issues in Damshung County. In 1999, Liu Liang was transferred to Chushur County to work in its Agriculture & Animal Husbandry Bureau, but after a year or so he switched to a desk job in the office of the Chushur Communist Party branch.

In 2003 he made the jump up to the Lhasa Municipality level in its Propaganda Department rising over ten years to become a Deputy Head of the Department. In August of 2013, Liu Liang was appointed a Deputy Party Secretary of Cheng-guan District's Party Standing Committee as well as Party Secretary and Head of Cheng-guan's Government administration. (See additional comments on Liu Liang in the Cheng-guan District Government section).

WANG WANQING

He is Deputy Party Secretary, Executive Deputy Head of Government, and a Beijing Aid Tibet Corps cadre

Ethnicity: Han Chinese

Wang Wanqing is a 47 year old, Beijing Aid Tibet Corps Han Chinese cadre. He is the leader of all the Beijing Aid Tibet cadres working in the Cheng-guan District.

Prior to arriving in Tibet in 2013, he was Deputy Director of the Development and Reform Commission in the East City District (东城区) of Beijing. Earlier in his career, following admission to the Communist Party in 1996, he had exposure to Procuratorate work and Party Organization Department work in another district of Beijing. (See additional comments on Wang Wanqing in the Cheng-guan District Government section).

DORJEE

He is Deputy Party Secretary, Party Secretary of the Bharkor Old City Management Committee.

Ethnicity: Tibetan

Comment: Dorjee is a Tibetan cadre who has responsibility for everything that concerns the Jokhang and Barkhor area of Lhasa. He is the Party Secretary of the "Barkhor Old City Management Committee"

NYIMA TSERING

He is Executive Deputy Party Secretary, Party Secretary of the Cheng-guan District Political and Legal Committee, a Deputy Head of the Lhasa Municipality Public Security Bureau, and Head of the Cheng-guan District Public Security Bureau.

Ethnicity: Tibetan

Comment: Nyima Tsering is the most recent addition to the Cheng-guan District Party Standing Committee. His predecessor, SONAM TSERING who had been Party Secretary of the Cheng-guan District Political and Legal Committee resigned after being promoted up to the Lhasa Municipality level as Head of the Lhasa Land & Resources Bureau.

CHIME TSERING

He is Deputy Secretary, Executive Deputy Head of the Cheng-guan District Government.

Ethnicity: Tibetan

Comment: On the District Party Standing Committee Chime Tsering seems to take responsibility for development projects which require legal and consensual land acquisition or land transfers. His name has been linked in 2013 and 2014 to preparations for a new Lhasa airport, a Lhasa electric tram system, the construction of a north ring road in Lhasa and the need for off-street car parking facilities at the Barkhor Commericial Market. He has also been involved in campaigns to eradicate the use of polluting fuels and all other carcinogenic substances in Lhasa. (See additional comments on Chime Tsering in the Cheng-guan District Government section).

YANG JIANHONG, Colonel

He is Member and Commander of the Cheng-guan People's Armed Police.

Ethnicity: Han Chinese

Comment: Colonel **Yang Jianhong,** in addition to being in charge of the local PAP organization, also heads the Cheng-guan District National Defense Mobilization Committee and all the "Twin Support work" *shuang-yong gongzuo*) which seeks to improve the working relationship with the civilian population of Lhasa.

ZHANG SHANGFU

He is a Member and Cheng-guan Party Secretary in charge of Discipline Inspection

Comment: Zhang Shangfu is a 44 year old Han Chinese cadre from Gansu Province. He has been in Tibet for some time and has held appointments in Cheng-guan District for at least the last six years. His mandate is to manage the District's Discipline Inspection inspectors and prioritize the cases for them to investigate.

TSEYANG *(f)*

She is Member, Head of the Propaganda Department.

Ethnicity: Tibetan

Comment: Tseyang is tasked with matters that combine 'culture' with politics. She shoulders responsibility for promoting the Chinese Spiritual Civilization Movement in Cheng-guan. She also monitors culture-related broadcasting on radio and television and all cultural preservation work in Cheng-guan. She handles all District information directed at outside audiences. **Tseyang's** predecessor was a Han Chinese female cadre named Zhang Bifang who is today a Deputy Head of the Lhasa Municipality Propaganda Department and Director of its 'Spiritual Civilization' Office.

SHEN PENGLI

He is Member, Head of the Organization Department.

Ethnicity: Han Chinese

Comment: As head of the Party's Organization Department, Shen Pengli and his team closely monitor and assess the work of all cadres in the District. Promotions, transfers and the occasional demotion along with study sabbaticals in inland China all rely heavily on inputs from the Organization Department. Each cadre's personal file resides within the Organization Department. In addition Shen Pengli is seen frequently in the media at Party-building functions, activities involving worker, youth and women's associations, and state enterprise human resources events.

(1st on the left is Lhakpa Tsering)

LHAKPA TSERING

He is Member , Head of the United Front Department.

Ethnicity: Tibetan

Comment: Lhakpa Tsering provides assistance and support to **Ma Yongqing** who apparently takes the lead on ethnic and religious affairs in the District. He also oversees the local Industry & Commerce Federation. Prior to joining the District Standing Committee, he was Head of the Housing and Urban/Rural Construction Bureau in Cheng-guan. No clear photo of him has so far been found.

DAWA PHUNTSOK

He is Member, and a Deputy Head of Government.

Ethnicity: Tibetan

Comment: Dawa Phuntsok is seldom if ever mentioned in the media so no meaningful impression of him can be put together at this time. When he has appeared it has been in a support role briefing visiting delegations on the progress and problems of Cheng-guan's major projects.

(Comment: While clearly there is more than one Tibetan official with this name, a 'DAWA PHUNTSOG' mentioned in 2011 as being the Chief Justice in Nyemo County could be this DAWA PHUNTSOG in a previous posting.)

LI HUAIWEI

He is Chairman of the Cheng-guan District CPPCC.

Ethnicity: Han Chinese

Li Huaiwei is presented here because he is a member of the Chinese Communist Party and because he represents the fourth pillar of the Cheng-guan District political establishment, i.e., the Chairman of the District's Chinese People's Political Consultative Conference (which otherwise is not listed here). The other three pillars, **Guo Guo** (Communist Party), **Ma Yongqing** (People's Congress) and **Liu Liang** (Government), have already been listed.

Li Huaiwei is now 62 years old, so this Chairmanship likely will be his last appointment before retirement. Li Huaiwei was born in Kanlho Prefecture (Gannan Tibetan Autonomous Prefecture, Gansu Province) where he studied and earned a degree in Veterinary Medicine. His career began at the age of 23 when he was assigned veterinary assistant work at a pastoral station in Lingtai County along the border between Gansu and Shaanxi Provinces. In 1979, he was transferred to Damshung County in the TAR, first as a working field vet and then in the mid-1980s as a cadre in the Damshung Animal Husbandry Bureau. In 1992, Li's professional focus changed when he was appointed Deputy Head of the Damshung County Party Propaganda Department. This assignment lasted barely a year before another change saw Li Huaiwei take over as Director of the Damshung Communist Party's Administrative Office. In 1995 he joined the Damshung Party Standing Committee and was named Head of its Propaganda Department. Five years later in 2000, he assumed the same portfolio for the Cheng-guan District Standing Committee. 2005 saw him keep his Cheng-guan Standing Committee membership, relinquish the Propaganda Department position but add Chairmanship of the Cheng-guan CPPCC as well as Party Secretary of the Communist Party cell within the CPPCC. Finally in the summer of 2006, Li Huaiwei shed his Standing Committee membership, maintaining only the Cheng-guan District CPPCC roles and continues in this capacity to this day.

LHASA MUNICIPALITY COUNTY PARTY LEADERS

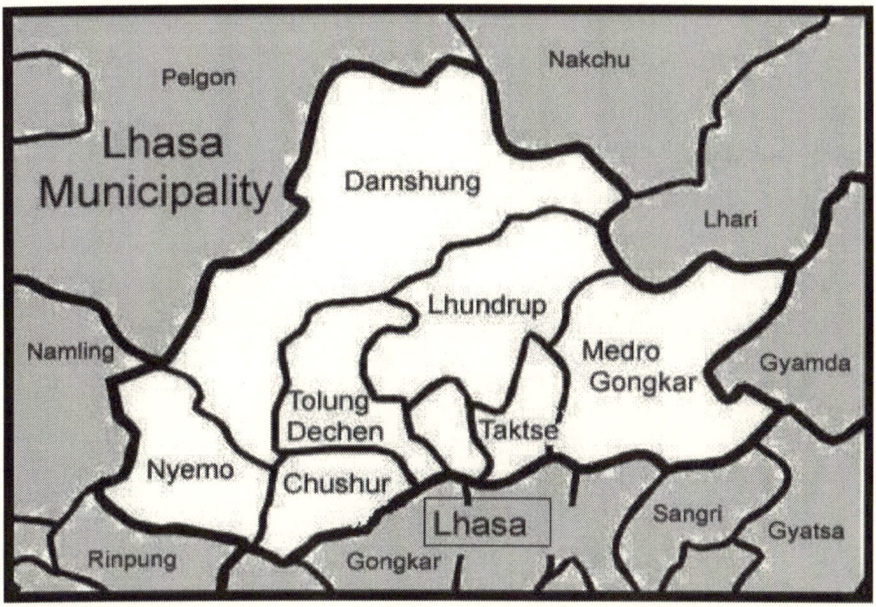

Chushur County

Party Secretary	**PENG Yitao**	(**Ethnicity**: Han Chinese)
Govt Head	**SUN Baoxiang**	(**Ethnicity**: Tibetan)

Damshung County

Party Secretary	**ZHANG Zheng**	(**Ethnicity**: Han Chinese)
Govt Head	**TENZING Nyima**	(**Ethnicity**: Tibetan)

Lhundrup County

Party Secretary	**ZHAO Tao**	(**Ethnicity**: Tibetan)
Govt Head	**TSERING Dondup**	(**Ethnicity**: Tibetan)

Medrogongkar County

Party Secretary	**YAN Yingjun**	(**Ethnicity**: Han Chinese)
Govt Head:	**LIN Sheng**	(**Ethnicity**: Tibetan)

Nyemo County

Party Secretary	**FAN Yonghong**	(**Ethnicity**: Han)
Govt Head	**PHULCHUNG**	(**Ethnicity**: Tibetan)

Taktse County

Party Secretary	**XU Shenfeng**	(**Ethnicity**: Han Chinese)
Govt Head	**NGO Tsering**	(**Ethnicity**: Tibetan)

Tolung Dechen County

Party Secretary	**CHEN Xiansen**	(**Ethnicity**: Han Chinese)
Govt Head	**AN Yangjin**	(**Ethnicity**: Tibetan)

A pattern evident in the counties of Lhasa Municipality is that when the county Party Secretary is a Han Chinese –regardless of whether he/she is an Aid Tibet cadre – the county Government Administrator will be a Tibetan. It works in the opposite way as well. When the Party Secretary is Tibetan – as in Cheng-guan District – the Government Administrator will usually be a Han Chinese. There is only one exception and this is Lhundrup County where both are Tibetan.

It is interesting that in the cases where the county Party Secretary is a Chinese Aid Tibet cadre, the county Government Administrator is not only a Tibetan but a Tibetan who has been in the post for a long time and possesses an intimate knowledge of the county. It appears that this Tibetan Government Administrator is expected to take his Chinese colleague under his wing and guide him in almost a mentor/protégée relationship.

BACKGROUNDS OF COUNTY PARTY SECRETARIES

Chushur County

PENG YITAO

He is Party Secretary

Ethnicity: Han Chinese

Peng Yitao's first media mention dates from Autumn 2010 when his position was listed as Deputy Party Secretary of the Cheng-guan District (urban/suburban Lhasa). Shortly thereafter he was concurrently appointed , Head of Government administration for the Cheng-guan District directly handling the local branch of the State Commission on Public Sector Reform, the Administrative Investigation Bureau, the Finance Bureau, the National Defense Mobilization Committee, the local Committee on Aging and liaison for all tax matters. In early 2012, Peng Yitao took a temporary leave of absence to become Deputy General Manager of the Lhasa Land Investment & Development Group Ltd. and office director of the Government small group established to get the company started. In mid-2013 Peng Yitao was back on track with his political career. He was appointed to fill the very big shoes of Zhou Guangzhi, the most successful and high profile of recent County Party Secretaries in the TAR. Zhou Guangzhi had been sent from Taizhou City in Jiangsu Province and spent six years (two Aid Tibet contract periods) in Chushur County. He oversaw the completion of a large number of development projects with minimum social disruption and maximum community support from the county's 35,000 population. For the last 20 years, Han Chinese cadres from Taizhou City have been in charge of Chushur's development projects, but Zhou Guangzhi's work was described as the most successful bringing national awards for its industrial park and its model farming area in Cai-na Rural Township. Peng Yitao took over Zhou Guangzhi's position of Party Secretary when the latter returned to Jiangsu Province. Unfortunately there is not enough biographical material on Peng Yitao to determine whether he too is an Aid Tibet Corps cadre or simply a Han Chinese who plans to spent his career in the TAR. Peng Yitao, however, does not appear to come from Taizhou City, which is a big change in Chushur County official circles.

Damshung County

ZHANG ZHENG

He is Party Secretary

Ethnicity: Han Chinese

Zhang Zheng is not an Aid Tibet contract cadre from Beijing or Jiangsu Province. He is a 42 year old Sichuanese whose entire 17 year career to date has been spent in the TAR. He began as a teacher, first in Nyemo County where he joined the Communist Party and later in Lhasa. After five years he left teaching and went to work for the Lhasa Procuratorate where he rose to be an Investigator and a Section Chief in the justice system. In the summer of 2008, Zhang Zheng was transferred to Damshung County as head of its Organization Department. After two years he was made a Deputy Party Secretary on the Damshung Standing Committee. In early 2011 at the age of 37 Zhang Zheng was brought back to Lhasa as Party Secretary of the municipality's Communist Youth League. This was a two year interim position after which he returned to Damshung County in July, 2013 as its Party Secretary.

Lhundrub County

ZHAO TAO

He is Party Secretary

Ethnicity: Tibetan

Zhao Tao is a 45-year old Tibetan who lists his ancestral home as Tai-an City in Shandong Province. Since this area supplied soldiers to the 18th Army, it is possible Zhao Tao's father arrived in Tibet with the PLA and his mother is Tibetan. Zhao Tao was born and raised in Tibet, and when he reached the age of consent he probably chose the Tibetan nationality of his mother.

He studied Economic Planning & Statistics at the Tibetan Nationality Institute in Shaanxi Province. Upon his return to the TAR he began his career in the Lhasa Municipal Procuratorate as an assistant judicial officer. It was at this juncture that he joined the Communist Party. He gradually rose in the Procuratorate as an Investigator and then head of the Prosecution Section. During this time he took distance education courses in Law from Tsinghua University in Beijing.

In 2002, Zhao Tao was named head of the Cheng-guan District (urban/suburban Lhasa) Procuratorate. Six years later in 2008 he moved back up to the Lhasa Municipal level as Deputy Party Secretary and head of the Lhasa Municipal Justice Department.

In 2010 Zhao Tao's career took a new direction. He was appointed Deputy Party Secretary and head of the Nyemo County Government. In the late spring of 2013 he was promoted to Party Secretary and moved to Lhundrub County where there is a huge hydro power infrastructure project in progress. Also Lhundrub County with 38 monasteries had been the most unstable of the Lhasa counties after March 14, 2008, so a strong and knowledgeable Tibetan hand was needed at the helm of the Party rather than a newly arrived Aid Tibet Han cadre. This was true of the county Government as well. Zhao Tao seems to have a promising future in front of him.

Maldrogongkar County

YAN YINGJUN

He is Party Secretary

Ethnicity: Han Chinese

Yan Yingjun is a 44 year old, Jiangsu Aid-Tibet Corps, Han nationality cadre who arrived in Tibet from Nanjing in the summer of 2013. As a teenager Yan Yingjun first went to work at the Nanjing No.3 Steel Mill starting as an apprentice technician. In 1997 he switched to government work in what then was Jiangning County, a distant suburb of Nanjing. After becoming a Party member in 2000 he briefly led the Communist Youth League in Jiangning. As Nanjing grew and spread, Jiangning became a District of the city. For many years Yan Yingjun did office administration while also becoming heavily involved in creation of the Binjiang Economic Development Zone. In 2007, Yan Yingjun was promoted to Party Secretary of Lukou Township within the Jiangning District. Four years later he was a member of the Jiangning Standing Committee, its office Director and head of its Propaganda Department. When Yan Yingjun joined the Jiangsu Aid Tibet Corps he was a Deputy Party Secretary and had worked for 17 straight years in Jiangning County/District which then would have been considered a somewhat small urban/rural community of a little less than one million in population.

Nyemo County

FAN YONGHONG

Party Secretary

Ethnicity: Han Chinese

Fan Yonghong is a 46- year old, Beijing Aid Tibet Corps, Han Chinese cadre who arrived in Tibet in the summer of 2013. His family originally is from Shandong Province, but he attended Beijing University where he earned a MA degree in Commercial & Industrial Management. The next 20 years were spent in the Haidian District of Beijing in various environmental, health care, industrial, agricultural products and general economic development roles. He was involved in the formation of two state-owned enterprise companies marketing Haidian products, and for the five years prior to arriving in Tibet was Party Secretary of one of the companies, the **Yuyuantan Corporation** (玉渊潭农工商总公司), an investment company dealing with hotels, commercial property and building materials.

Tagtse County

XU SHENFENG

He is Party Secretary

Ethnicity: Han Chinese

Xu Shenfeng is a 40 year old, Jiangsu Aid-Tibet Corps, Han nationality cadre who arrived in Tibet in the early summer of 2013. His ancestral home is in Hubei Province, but he attended and graduated from the Shipping School of the East China Institute of Technology in Jiangsu Province. Before he arrived in Tibet his entire 19 year career was spent working his way up through increasingly higher administrative levels of Zhenjiang City, located between Shanghai and Nanjing on the Yangtze River. From 2011-2013, Xu Shenfeng was in charge of an Economic Development zone in one of Zhenjiang City's townships.

Toelung Dechen County

CHEN XIANSEN

He is Party Secretary

Ethnicity: Han Chinese

Chen Xiansen is a 41- year old, Beijing Aid-Tibet Corps, Han nationality cadre who arrived in Tibet in mid-2013. His ancestral home is in Henan Province, but he attended the Chinese People's Public Security University in Beijing from where he graduated. The first seven years of his career were spent working in the Public Security Bureau (PSB) in the Xicheng District of Beijing. Chen Xiansen then switched to China Youth League work in the same district while simultaneously earning a MA degree from Beijing University in Government Public Affairs. His most recent three year period of work prior to leaving for Tibet was as a government and Party administrator of a large neighborhood work committee in Beijing's East City District. Arriving in Toelung Dechen County with Chen Xiansen were three other Beijing Aid Tibet Corps cadres who similarly assumed senior county positions in the Party and Government: (1) **CHEN**

Jianmin (陈建民) who became a Deputy Party Secretary & the Executive Deputy Head of Government, (2) **LOU Xiangfeng** (娄相峰) who became a Deputy Head of Government and (3) **YAN Tao** (闫涛) who became another Deputy Head of Government and the Director of Toelung Dechen's Industrial Park Management Committee.

Note: **CHEN Xiansen's** predecessor as Party Secretary was also a Beijing Aid Tibet Corps cadre named **SUN Derui** (孙德锐). This practice has been a common theme at the municipality, prefecture and county levels during the twenty plus years of the Aid Tibet program.

NGARI (CH: ALI) ADMINISTRATIVE DISTRICT (AD)

The Ngari (Ch: Ali) Administrative District (AD), borders India, with headquarters at Gar County. The famous Hindu pilgrim centres of Mansarovar and Mount Kailash are located in the region. The border trade post of Burang, which is used to conduct trade with India and Nepal and the trading post of Shipkila are in this prefecture. The total length of its border is 1,116 km, with 57 passes. The AD stretches 600 km from east to west and measures 550 km from north to south, covering a total area of 3,30,000 sq. km. It has a total population of 95,465, with a density of 0.23 people per sq. km. This is the largest AD in Tibet in terms of geographic area, with the least density of population. The number of peasants and herdsmen totals 58,807, or 85.2 percent of the total population.

Ngari Gunsa Airport is a dual-use military and civil airport serving the town of Sengye Khabab in Ngari Prefecture, in the southwest of the Tibet Autonomous Region near the Indian border. It started operations on 1 July 2010, becoming the fourth civil airport in Tibet after Lhasa, Nyingchi, and Chamdo airports.

Situated at 4,274 m (14,022 ft) above sea level, Gunsa Airport is the fourth highest airport in the world after Chamdo Bangda Airport (elevation 4,334 m (14,219 ft), Kangding Airport (elevation 4,280 m (14,042 ft)) and Nagchu Dangring, which was supposed to open for use in 2015 but has not been completed as yet. Once completed, Nagchu Dangring will be the highest airport in the world at 4,436 m (14,554 ft)). Gunsa airport has a 4,500-meter runway. It is expected to handle 120,000 passengers by 2020. Construction began in May 2007 and cost an estimated 1.65 billion yuan (US$ 241.22 million).

Counties under Ali AD:

Gar County

Burang County

Tsamda County

Rutog County

Gergye County

Gertse County

Tsochen

NGARI PARTY COMMITTEE

Deputy Secretaries of Ngari Party Committee

PEMA WANGDUE

Ethnicity: Tibetan

Previous Designation: Director of TAR Water Resource Department, Chief Commissioner of Ngari Administrative Commissioner and Deputy Secretary of Ngari Prefectural Committee and Chief Commissioner of Ngari Prefecture.

Current Designation: Promoted to Party Secretary of the Ngari Party Committee in 2015 and reportedly the youngest ethnic minority party secretary. He is 51 years old. He replaced Wan Chaoqi (Ethnicity: Han Chinese)

CUI TAIPING

Year of Birth: August 1965 in Gaocheng County of Hebei Province.

Ethnicity: Han Chinese

Year of Joining CCP: December 1985

Education: Graduated in Law from Political Department of China Youth College in July 1984.

Previous Designation: Party Secretary of Rutog County of Ngari Prefecture.

Current Designation: Deputy Secretary of Communist Party of Ngari Prefectural Committee since July 2013.

PHUNTSOK

Ethnicity: Tibetan

Previous Designation: Vice-Commissioner of Ngari and Nagchu

Current Designation: Deputy Secretary of Communist Party of Ngari (Ch: Ali) and Vice-Commissioner of Ngari Prefecture since 2011.

LOBSANG TENDAR

Year of Birth: July 15, 1954 in Burang (Ch: Pulan) County of Ngari Prefecture.

Ethnicity: Tibetan

Previous Designation: Vice-Chairman of TAR People's Congress Financial and Economic Committee till March 2011.

Current Designation: Deputy Secretary of Politics and Law Committee of Ngari Prefecture, Secretary of Police Department of Ngari Prefecture and Deputy Secretary of Communist Party of Ngari since December 2012.

YANG CHENG

PLA Senior Colonel

Ethnicity: Han Chinese

Current Designation: Deputy Secretary of Communist Party of Ngari and Political Commissar of Ngari (Ali) Military Sub-District.

LIU GANG

Ethnicity: Han Chinese

Current Designation: Deputy Secretary of Ngari Prefectural Committee and Secretary of Ngari Discipline Committee.

TENZIN PHUNTSOK

Ethnicity: Tibetan

Previous Designation: Secretary General and Vice-Commissioner of Ngari Administrative Office.

Current Designation: Deputy Secretary of Communist Party of Ngari and Chairman of Ngari Propaganda Department.

LUI YAO CHANG

Ethnicity: Han Chinese

Previous Designation: Deputy Director of Nagchuk (Ch: Nagqu) Organization Department.

Current Designation: Deputy Secretary of Communist Party of Ngari and Director of Ngari Organization Department since 2011.

TOPCHEN

Ethnicity: Tibetan

Previous Designation: Chairman of Ngari Propaganda Department

Current Designation: Vice-Commissioner of Ngari Administrative Office and Chairman of Ngari United Front Work Department.

WANG BIAO

Ethnicity: Han Chinese

Previous Designation: Governor of Zhenping County of Shanxi Province.

Current Designation: Standing Committee Member of Communist Party of Ngari and Vice-Commissioner of Ngari Administrative office.

RIN CHEN ZHEN

Ethnicity: Han Chinese

Previous Designation: Governor of Gegye County of Ngari Prefecture and Vice-Chairman of Ngari CPPCC.

Current Designation: Secretary General and Standing Committee member of Ngari Communist Party of China.

GOMPA SUM

Ethnicity: Tibetan

Previous Designation: Governor of Amdo and Sog County of Nagchu (Ch: Nagqu) Prefecture.

Current Designation: Vice-Commissioner of Ngari Administration Office and standing member of Communist Party of Ngari.

Ngari/Ali Prefecture People's Congress

SHAWO DAWA

Chairman

Year of Birth: 1954 in Gertse County of Ngari

Ethnicity: Tibetan

Previous Designation: Party Secretary of Tsochen County of Ngari Prefecture.

Current Designation: Director of Ngari Discipline Inspection Committee, Vice- Chairman of Ngari Prefecture People's Congress since 2008 and promoted to Chairmanship of Ngari Prefecture People's Congress in 2012.

Vice-Chairmen of Ngari/Ali Prefecture People's Congress

GONPO

Ethnicity: Tibetan

Previous Designation: Chairman of Ngari Propaganda Department

Current Designation: Vice-Chairman of Ngari Prefecture People's Congress since 2011.

DAWA TSOMO *(f)*

Ethnicity: Tibetan

Previous Designation: Director of Ngari Prefecture Work Committee

Current Designation: Vice-Chairman of Ngari Prefecture People's Congress since 2005.

ZHANG WENZHAO

Ethnicity: Han Chinese

Previous Designation: Party Secretary of Gertse County of Ngari Prefecture.

Current Designation: Vice-Chairman of Ngari Prefecture People's Congress since July 2012.

Ngari (Ch: Ali) Prefecture Administrative Commission

PEMA WANGDUE

Chief Commissioner

Ethnicity: Tibetan

(See page 102 for his Bio-details)

Vice-Commissioners

PHUNTSOK
Ethnicity: Tibetan

WANG BIAO
Ethnicity: Han Chinese

GOMPA SUM
Ethnicity: Tibetan

(See Page 103 and 105 respectively for bio-details)

CHENQING XIA *(f)*

Ethnicity: Han Chinese

Previous Designation: Director of Ngari Development Committee

Current Designation: Vice-Commissioner of Ngari Administrative Commission since 2011.

HU JUN

Ethnicity: Han Chinese

Previous Designation:

Current Designation: Vice-Commissioner of Nagri Administrative Commission since end of 2011.

THUPTEN TSERING

Ethnicity: Tibetan

Previous Designation: Governor of Burang County of Ngari Prefecture

Current Designation: Vice-Commissioner of Ngari Administrative Commission since 2011.

YANG CHUN

Ethnicity: Han Chinese

Previous Designation: Director of Ngari Social Development and Change Committee

Current Designation: Vice-Commissioner of Ngari Administrative Commission since 2012.

YAO YONGQIANG

Ethnicity: Han Chinese

Current Designation: Vice-Commissioner of Ngari Administrative Commission since 2012

SONAM TSETAN

Ethnicity: Tibetan

Previous Designation: Deputy Director and Secretary of Communist Party of Ngari Agriculture and Animal Husbandry Department.

Current Designation: Vice-Commissioner of Ngari Administrative Commission since 2012.

GEQING MIN

Ethnicity: Han Chinese

Year of Birth: 1970 in Qinghai Province

Current Designation: Vice-Commissioner of Ngari Administrative Commission.

LIU JIANWEI

Ethnicity: Han Chinese

Current Designation: Vice-Commissioner of Ngari Administrative Commission.

ZHANG HUIMING

Ethnicity: Han Chinese

Year of Birth: 1940 in Burang County of Ngari Prefecture

Current Designation: Vice-Commissioner of Ngari Administrative Commission since 2013.

Ngari/Ali Prefecture People's Political Consultative Conference (PPCC)

Chairman: LOBSANG PALMO *(f)*

Ethnicity: Tibetan

Previous Designation: Chairman of Ngari Women's Federation.

Current Designation: Vice Chairman of Ngari PPCC

KHANGNEYPA PASSANG

Ethnicity: Han Chinese

Year of Birth: 1940 in Burang County of Ngari Prefecture.

Current Designation: Standing Member of PPCC and Vice Chairman of Ngari PPCC

PEMA TSERING

Ethnicity: Tibetan

Current Designation: Vice Chairman of Ngari PPCC

LOBSANG SAMTEN

Ethnicity: Tibetan

Current Designation: Vice Chairman of Ngari PPCC.

LOGYA TSERING

Ethnicity: Tibetan

Current Designation: Vice Chairman of Ngari PPCC

REWA

Ethnicity: Tibetan

Current Designation: Vice Chairman of Ngari PPCC since 2012

LI YIJIAN

Ethnicity: Han Chinese

Current Designation: Vice Chairman of Ngari PPCC since 2012

SHENG JUNKAO

Ethnicity: Han Chinese

Current Designation: Vice Chairman of Ngari PPCC

Shigatse (Ch: Xigaze) Administrative District (AD)

The Shigatse Administrative District, with headquarters at Shigatse, covers 1, 76, 000 sq km. The AD has a 1,507 km long border with Nepal, Bhutan and India, with 17 posts and border trade centres situated along its length. The AD has a population of 703,292. The 253-km Lhasa- Shigatse Railway line was started in September 2010 and completed in July 2014. The line was formally opened in August 2014 and includes 14 stations. The project had a budget of 13.3 billion yuan. The completion of this project potentially extends the network further west and south into Nepal and to Yadong County, close to the border with Sikkim, India.

Shigatse Peace Airport began operations on 30 October 2010 after an Airbus A319 landed safely, making it Tibet's fifth commercial airport. It is located 43 km from Samzhubzê (Samdhub Tsechu) District at Jiangdang Village at an altitude of 3,782 metres. The airport is designed to handle up to 230,000 passengers annually by 2020.

Counties under Shigatse AD:

Samdhub Tsechu

Namling

Gyangze

Tingri

Sakya

Lhatse

Ngyamring

Xaitongmoin

Panam

Rinpung

Kangmar

Dinggyê

Zhongba

Dromo

Gyirong

Nyalam

Saga

Gamba

Communist Party of Shigatse Prefecture (Changed to City in 2014)

TENZIN NAMGYAL
Party Secretary
Ethinicity: Tibetan

(See Page 51 for bio-details)

Shigatse Municipal Party Committee (16 members)

LIU SHAN

Ethnicity: Han Chinese

Current Designation: CCP Shigatse Municipal Committee and Chairman of Shigatse Municipal People's Congress.

FANG JIANGUO

Ethnicity: Han Chinese

Designation: Member of CCP Shigatse Municipal Committee and Military Commander.

TASHI TSERING

Ethnicity: Tibetan

Designation: Member of CCP Shigatse Muncipal Committee and Head of Discipline Committee.

ZHU JIANG

Ethnicity: Han Chinese

Designation: Member of CCP Shigatse Municipal Committee, Deputy Secretary of the Politics and Law Committee and Party Secretary of Municipal Public Security Bureau.

LHAKPA PHUNTSOK

Ethnicity: Tibetan

Designation: Member of CCP Shigatse Municipal Committee and Head of United Front Work Department (UFWD).

YANG KUN

Ethnicity: Han Chinese

Designation: Member of CCP Shigatse Municipal Committee and Head of Organization Department.

LEI JINCHANG

Ethnicity: Han Chinese

Current Designation: Secretary General of Shigatse Municipal Committee.

Note: Increased membership from 13 to 16

Dismissed members are: Ngodup Dolma (Ethnicity: Tibetan), Phurbu (Ethnicity: Tibetan), Sonam Tashi (Ethnicity: Tibetan).

CCP Shigatse Municipal People's Congress

LIU SHAN

Ethnicity: Han Chinese

Current Designation: CCP Shigatse Municipal Committee member and Chairman of Shigatse Municipal People's Congress.

Note: Replaced Thundel (Ethnicity: Tibetan)

WANG YANGTIAN

Ethnicity: Han Chinese

Designation: Deputy Chairman of Shigatse People's Congress.

WANG PING

Ethnicity: Han Chinese

Designation: Deputy Chairman of Shigatse Standing Committee and Party Secretary of Nyalam County of Shigatse.

PA ZHU

Ethnicity: Han Chinese

Designation: Deputy Chairman of Shigatse Standing Committee and Party Secretary Kyirong County.

PASSANG DORJEE

Ethnicity: Tibetan

Designation: Deputy Chairman of Shigatse Standing Committee and Party Secretary Namling of County.

ZHAO XIAOZHU

Ethnicity: Han Chinese

Designation: Deputy Chairman of Shigatse Municipal People's Congress, Deputy Secretary of Municipal Party Committee's Organization Department and Party Secretary of Shigatse City and Social Council.

XIA JIA

Ethnicity: Han Chinese

Designation: Vice Chairman of Shigatse Municipal People's Congress.

P: S- Number of members increased from three earlier to nine now including the Chairman.

Shigatse Municipal People's Government (Total member-12)

PASSANG

Ethnicity: Tibetan

Designation: Deputy Mayor of Shigatse Municipal People's Government.

SAMDRUP TSERING

Ethnicity: Tibetan

Designation: Deputy Mayor of Shigatse Municipal People's Government.

Note: Dismissed Paldon (Ethnicity: Tibetan), Phurbu Samdrup (Ethnicity: Tibetan), Li Chezhang (Ethnicity: Han Chinese).

Shigatse Municipal PPCC (10 members)

PHURBU

Ethnicity: Tibetan

Designation: Chairman of Shigatse Municipal PPCC. (Replaced Chungpa, Ethnicity: Tibetan).

SONAM DAKPA

Ethnicity: Tibetan

Designation: Vice Chairman of Shigatse PPCC.

ZHAO ZHANWEN

Ethnicity: Han Chinese

Designation: Vice Chairman of Shigatse PPCC.

DAWA DAMDUL

Ethnicity: Tibetan

Designation: Vice Chairman of Shigatse PPCC.

TSERING DHONDUP

Ethnicity: Tibetan

Designation: Vice Chairman of Shigatse PPCC and District Mayor of Samdruptse District.

GYADOR

Ethnicity: Tibetan

Designation: :Vice Chairman of Shigatse PPCC and Deputy Secretary of Sakya County.

PEMBA

Ethnicity: Tibetan

Designation: Vice Chairman of Shigatse and Party Secretary of Shigatse Water Conservation Bureau.

SONG ZE (f)

Ethnicity: Han Chinese

Designation: Vice Chairman of Shigatse and Party Secretary of Shigatse letter office.

Note: Membership decreased from 12 to 10.

Dismissed members are: Salung Phuntsok (Ethnicity: Tibetan), Li Li Lan (Ethnicity: Han Chinese), Thukten Tsewang (Ethnicity: Tibetan), Dorjee (Ethnicity: Tibetan), Hong Chenze (Ethnicity: Han Chinese), Lhakpa Phuntsok (Ethnicity: Tibetan), Wangyal Tsering (Ethnicity: Tibetan), Sonam (Ethnicity: Tibetan), Lobsang Soepa (Ethnicity: Tibetan).

ZHANG HONGPAO

Ethnicity: Han Chinese

Previous Designation: Deputy Secretary of Communist Party of Shigatse, Secretary of Shigatse Discipline Committee, Secretary of Shigatse Public Security Bureau.

Current Designation: Deputy Secretary of Communist Party of Shigatse and Chief Commissioner of Shigatse Administrative Commission since February, 2015.

ZHAO ZHIYUAN

Year of Birth: 1955 in Haidong Province of China

Ethnicity: Han Chinese

Previous Designation: Deputy Secretary of Haidong Province of China

Current Designation: Deputy Secretary of Communist Party of Shigatse Prefecture, Vice-Commissioner of Shigatse Administrative Commission and Staff of Tibet Aid Department since.

DIAJING BIN

Year of Birth: 1970 in Jiangsu Province of PRC

Ethnicity: Han Chinese

Current Designation: Deputy Secretary of CCP, Shigatse (Ch: Xigaze) and Tibet Aid official.

TRINLAY NYIMA

Ethnicity: Tibetan

Current Designation: Secretary General and Standing Committee Member of Communist Party of Shigatse.

HAN YANG

Year of Birth:1972

Ethnicity: Han Chinese

Current Designation: Deputy Secretary of Communist Party of Shigatse, Vice Commissioner of Shigatse Prefecture and Tibet Aid Official.

WANG BO

Place of Birth: Haidong Provice of PRC

Ethnicity: Han Chinese

Current Designation: Deputy Secretary and Standing Committee member of Communist Party of Shigatse.

Shigatse City People's Congress
Vice Chairmen of Shigatse People's Congress

GYATSO

Ethnicity: Tibetan

Previous Designation: Chairman of Dongpa County of Shigatse

Current Designation: Vice Chairman of Shigatse People's Congress since 2010.

NYIMA TSANG

Ethnicity: Tibetan

Current Designation: Vice Chairman of Shigatse People's Congress since January 2013.

SHAKYA

Ethnicity: Tibetan

Designation: Vice Chairman of Shigatse Municipal People's Congress since February, 2015.

Shigatse City People's Government

TANG HONGPAO

Ethnicity: Han Chinese

Previous Designation: Deputy Secretary of Communist Party of Shigatse, Secretary of Shigatse Discipline Committee, Secretary of Shigatse Public Security Bureau.

Current Designation: Deputy Secretary of Communist Party of Shigatse and Chief Commissioner of Shigatse Administrative Commission since December 2012.

Vice Chairmen of Shigatse Administrative Commission

KARMA LOCHUNG

Ethnicity: Tibetan

Previous Designation: Director and Deputy Secretary of Shigatse Wealth and Resource Department from the end of 2007 to 2011.

Current Designation: Vice-Mayor of Shigatse Prefecture since the end of 2011.

TSERING YANGZOM *(f)*

Ethnicity: Tibetan

Previous Designation: Director of Shigatse Land Department and Governor of Dingye County since 2007

Current Designation: Deputy Mayor of Shigatse Prefecture since 2012.

ZHENG LIANWU

Ethnicity: Han Chinese

Year of Birth: 1966 in Henan Province

Previous Designation: Deputy Secretary of Jiaozhou Prefecture of Henan Province.

Current Designation: Vice Mayor of Shigatse Prefecture and Tibet Aid Official since July 2013.

ZHANG XIUWU

Ethnicity: Han Chinese

Year of Birth: 1974

Previous Designation: Party Secretary of Taiyuan City of Shanxi Province from 2011-2013.

Current Designation: Deputy Mayor of Shigatse Prefecture and Party Secretary Sakya County since July 2013.

YAO CHANGYU

Ethnicity: Han Chinese

Year of Birth: 1967 Lishang County of Hunan Province.

Previous Designation: Governor and Party Secretary of a County in Hunan Province from 2010-2013.

Current Designation: Deputy Mayor of Shigatse Prefecture since July 2013.

GAN LIQUAN

Ethnicity: Han Chinese

Previous Designation: Party Secretary of Fulin Town of Chongqing City.

Current Designation: Deputy Mayor of Shigatse Prefecture since July 2013.

ZHAO ZHIYUAN

Ethinicity: Han Chinese

TRINLAY NYIMA

Ethnicity: Tibetan

HAN YANG

Ethnicity: Han Chinese

(See page 118 for bio-details)

People's Political Consultative Conference of Shigatse City (PPCC)

Vice Chairmen of Shigatse PPCC

GYALTSE NYANDAK

Year of Birth: November 1955 in Gyanze County of Shigatse

Ethnicity: Tibetan

Previous Designation: Vice Chairman of Democratic Management Committee of Tashi Lhunpo Monastery and TAR Buddhist Association.

Current Designation: Vice Chairman of PPCC Shigatse since 2012.

NORBU

Ethnicity: Tibetan

Previous Designation: Secretary of Shigatse Human Resource and Social Security Bureau

Current Designation: Vice Chairman of Shigatse PPCC.

ZHANG ZHUO

Year of Birth: 1962

Ethnicity: Han Chinese

Current Designation: Deputy Secretary of Communist Party of Shigatse and Vice-Chairman of CPPCC Shigatse.

SHANNAN (LOKHA) ADMINISTRATIVE DISTRICT

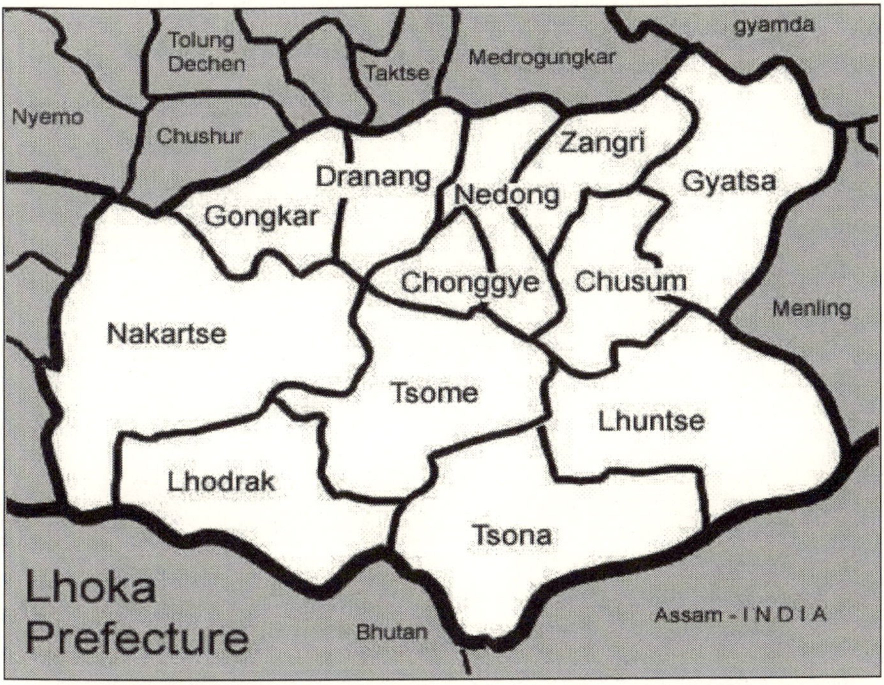

Shannan/Lhoka AD is located in the lower reaches of the Yarlung Tsangpo River south of the Kangdese Mountains (called the Nyenchen-tanglha Mountains on the Qinghai-Tibet Plateau). It is bounded by the capital city Lhasa to the north, Shigatse to the west, Nyingtri to the east, and India and Bhutan to the south. With an area of 73,500 sq. km and a land border over 600 km, it has great strategic importance and is China's southwestern border area. The AD has a population of 328,990. Gongga Airport is located in this AD.

Tsethang, the prefectural capital of Shannan (Lhoka), has a population of about 58,000, with between 10,000 to 18,000 Han Chinese. The Norbusa Chromite Mine in Shannan Prefecture has become a chromite production base. There are 88 lakes in the prefecture including Yamdrok Yumtso Lake.

Counties under Lhoka AD:

Nedong

Dranang

Gongkar

Zangri

Chonggye

Chu-Sum

Tsome

Lhodrak

Gyatsa

Lhuntse

Tsona

Nakartse

Communist Party of Shannan/Lhoka Administrative District

CHIME RINZIN

Party Secretary

Year of Birth: February 1958, Maldogongkar County of Lhasa

Ethnicity: Tibetan

Previous Designation: Party Secretary and Deputy Secretary of Trinkuchu (Ch: Chengguan) District of Lhasa from 2009-2011.

Current Designation: Party Secretary of Lhoka (Ch: Shannan) Prefecture since 2011.

Deputy Secretaries of Lhoka Administrative District

ZHANG YONGZE

Year of Birth: March 1969 in Quibei County of Yunnan Province.

Ethnicity: Han Chinese

Year of Joining CCP: July 1994

Education: Doctorate in Engineering from Sichuan Union University.

Previous Designation: Worked as Deputy Director, Deputy Secretary of TAR Environmental Protection Agency from 1998-2012.

Current Designation: Deputy Secretary of Lhoka Party Committee and Commissioner of Lhoka Prefecture since April 2012.

ZHANG MING

Year of Birth: October 1965 in Jiangsu Province

Ethnicity: Han Chinese

Previous Designation: Party Secretary and Standing Member of Shushan District Party Committee of Hefei County in Anhui Province of China from 2010-2013.

Current Designation: Deputy Secretary of Lhoka Party Committee and Tibet Aid Official.

HU DONGHAI

Year of Birth: January 1967 in Hubei Province

Ethnicity: Han Chinese

Previous Designation: Deputy Secretary General of Huanggang Prefecture and Party Secretary of Suizhou County of Hubei Province.

Current Designation: Vice-Commissioner and Standing Member of Lhoka Party Committee.

DANG ZONGLIAN *(f)*

Year of Birth: April 1963 in Gansu Province

Ethnicity: Han Chinese

Education: Post graduate from Central Party School

Year of Joining CCP: March 1984

Current Designation: Secretary of Commission for Discipline Inspection, Lhoka Prefecture and Standing Member of Lhoka Party Committee since September 2010.

JIGME

Year of Birth: September 1960 in Kham Bathang in Karze (Ch: Sichuan Province)

Ethnicity: Tibetan

Education: Post Graduate

Previous Designation: Party Secretary of Lhoka Prefecture, Member of Lhoka Police Department and Political and Legal Committee from December 2011 to February 2014.

Current Designation Deputy Secretary of Lhoka Party Committee, Secretary of Lhoka Political and Legal Committee and Regional Police Department respectively.

KARMA TENPA

Year of Birth: January 1963 in Phungyal County of Lhoka

Ethnicity: Tibetan

Year of Joining CCP: September 1982

Previous Designation: Vice-Commissioner of Civil Administration, Lhoka Prefecture from November 2009-January 2012.

Current Designation: Minister of Lhoka Propaganda Department and Standing Member of Lhoka Party Committee since January 2012.

BARDO

Year of Birth: June 1965 in Tsona County of Lhoka

Ethnicity: Tibetan

Year of Joining CCP: July 1982

Previous Designation: Party Secretary of Danang County of Lhoka from October 2010 to June 2012.

Current Designation: Director of Lhoka United Front Work Department (UFWD) and Standing member of Lhoka Party Committee since June 2012.

YONTEN

Year of Birth: December 1967 in Ngakartse County of Lhoka

Ethnicity: Tibetan

Previous Designation: Deputy Commissioner of Lhoka Prefecture from November 2009-April 2012.

Current Designation: Vice-Commissioner of Lhoka Prefecture and Standing Member of Lhoka Party Committee since February 2012.

JIANG TAIQIANG

Year of Birth: December 1961, in Ningxiang County of Hunan Province.

Ethnicity: Han Chinese

Year of Joining CCP: July 1983

Education: Graduate of Central Party School

Previous Designation: Deputy Secretary General of TAR Party Committee from January 2012-July 2012.

Current Designation: Secretary General of Lhoka Party Committee since July 2012.

BOJIAN CAI

Year of Birth: November 1965, in Hiyang County of Hunan Province

Ethnicity: Han Chinese

Year of Joining CCP: July 1984

Education Qualification: Post Graduate

Previous Designation: Director General of Hunan Information and Technology Office from January 2013 to August 2013.

Current Designation: Deputy Secretary of Lhoka Party Committee, Vice-Commissioner of Lhoka Prefecture and Tibet Aid Official.

WU WEI

Year of Birth: November 1964, Yangquan County of Shanxi Province.

Ethnicity: Han Chinese

Education Qualification: Post Graduate

Year of Joining CCP: July 1987

Previous Designation: Secretary of Nyingtri (Ch: Nyingchi) Commission for Discipline Inspection and Standing Member of Nyingtri Party Committee from January 2013-December 2014.

Current Designation: Secretary of Lhoka Commission for Discipline Inspection and Standing Member of Lhoka Party Committee since December 2014.

SHAO CHANG

Year of Birth: December 1964 in Shanghai.

Ethnicity: Tibetan

Year of Joining CCP: July 1985

Education Qualification: Post Graduate

Previous Designation: Director of TAR Organization

Department from May 2013 to February 2014.

Current Designation: Director of Organization Department of Lhoka and Standing Member of Lhoka Party Committee since February 2014.

ZHANG MING

Year of Birth: October 1965 in Jiangsu Province

Year of Joining CCP: October 1982

Education Qualification: Graduate

Ethnicity: Han Chinese

Previous Designation: Secretary of Huaibei Municipal Committee of Anhui Province from July 2013.

Current Designation: Standing Member of Huaibei Municipal Committee of Anhui Province of China and Deputy Secretary of Lhoka Party Committee since July 2013..

DINGZHE FENG

Year of Birth: February 1964 in Shaanxi Province of China

Ethnicity: Han Chinese

Previous Designation: Deputy Director at Department Level in Xi'an (Capital of Shaanxi Province) Government Office and Vice-Chairman of TAR People's Government from December 2012 to February 2014.

Current Designation: Deputy Secretary of Lhoka Prefecture at Department Level since February 2014.

Lhoka Prefecture People's Congress

ZHANG ZONGLIAN *(f)*

Chairwoman

Ethnicity: Han Chinese

Vice Chairmen of Lhoka People's Congress

KARMA LOBSANG

Year of Birth: March 1958 in Phungyal County of Lhoka Prefecture

Ethnicity: Tibetan

Education Qualification: Graduate in International Politics from Central Party School

Year of Joining CCP: January 1980

Previous Designation: Vice-Commissioner and member of Lhoka Administrative Office from August 2005-November 2009.

Current Designation: Vice-Chairman and Standing Member of Lhoka People's Congress since November 2011.

SHAO LIMIN

Year of Birth: February 1956 in Fujian County of Shanxi Province

Ethnicity: Han Chinese

Previous Designation: Party Secretary of Gyatsa County of Lhoka Prefecture from 2010-2012.

Current Designation: Vice-Chairman of Lhoka People's Congress since 2012.

TASHI GYATSO

Ethnicity: Tibetan

Previous Designation: Director of Lhoka Advisory Committee

Current Designation: Vice-Chairman of Lhoka People's Congress.

Lhoka Administrative Office

ZHANG YONGZE

Commissioner

Ethnicity: Han Chinese

(See Page 130 for bio-details)

Deputy Commissioners/Deputy Secretaries

YONTEN

Ethnicity: Tibetan

BOJIAN CAI

Ethnicity: Han Chinese

(See Page 127 and 128 respectively for their bio-details)

KE DONGHAI

Year of Birth: January 1967 in Hubei Province

Ethnicity: Han Chinese

Year of Joining CCP: July 1986

Education Qualification: Post Graduate

Previous Designation: Party Secretary of Chu-gsum County of Lhoka Prefecture of Tibet from July 2010 to July 2013.

Current Designation: Standing Member of Lhoka Party Committee and Vice-Commissioner of Lhoka Prefecture since July 2013.

YINWONG *(f)*

Year of Birth: October 1971 in Riwoche County of Chamdo Prefecture

Ethnicity: Tibetan

Year of Joining CCP: July 1994

Previous Designation: Deputy Secretary of TAR Communist

Youth League and Deputy Director of Import and Export Food Safety Bureau from October 2009-December 2012.

Current Designation: Vice-Commissioner of Lhoka Prefecture and Standing Member of Lhoka Party Committee since December 2012.

KELSANG

Year of Birth: February 1964 in Shethongmon County of Shigatse Prefecture.

Ethnicity: Tibetan

Year of Joining CCP: April 1984

Previous Designation: Deputy Secretary of Bomy County of Nyingtri Prefecture from April 2004-June 2011.

Current Designation: Vice-Commissioner of Lhoka Prefecture since June 2011.

YU CHANG

Ethnicity: Han Chinese

Eduction Qualification: Graduate from Central Party School

Year of Joining CCP: December 1978

Previous Designation: Vice-Commissioner of Nagchu Prefecture from April 2012-April 2013.

Current Designation: Vice-Commissioner of Lhoka Prefecture and Standing Member of Lhoka Party Committee since April 2013.

HUANGJIN CHENG

Year of Birth: April 1962 Wuxi County of Jiangsu Province

Ethnicity: Han Chinese

Education Qualification: Post Graduate

Year of Joining CCP: July 1984

Previous Designation: Director of TAR Department of Water Resources Planning Division, November 2011-December 2011.

Current Designation: Vice-Commissioner of Lhoka

Prefecture and Standing Member of Lhoka Party Committee since December 2011.

JI SHIDE

Year of Birth: May 1960 in Shandong Province

Ethnicity: Han Chinese

Education Qualification: Post Graduate

Year of Joining CCP: January 1978

Previous Designation: Director of Revenue Management Department of TAR from September 2004-January 2012

Current Designation: Vice-Commissioner of Lhoka Prefecture and Standing Member of Lhoka Party Committee since January 2012.

TENZIN

Year of Birth: September 1965 in Lhodak County of Lhoka Prefecture

Ethnicity: Tibetan

Education Qualification: Post Graduate

Year of Joining CCP: July 1987

Previous Designation: Deputy Secretary of Nyedong County People's Government, Lhoka Prefecture from September 2010 to April 2012.

Current Designation: Vice-Commissioner of Lhoka Prefecture and Standing Member of Lhoka Party Committee since April 2012.

ZHANGFU CHEN

Year of Birth: September 1962 in Tangshan City of Hebei Province

Ethnicity: Han Chinese

Education Qualification: Post Graduate

Year of Joining CCP: January 1985

Previous Designation: Director of TAR Development and Reform Commission and Deputy Secretary of Lhoka Party Committee from October 2004 to April 2012.

Current Designation: Vice-Commissioner of Lhoka Prefecture since April 2012.

WANGYOU HUA

Year of Birth: October 1970

Ethnicity: Han Chinese

Education Qualification: Post Graduate

Year of Joining CCP: July 1992

Previous Designation: Acting Mayor and Deputy Secretary of Henan Province Party Committee from September 2009-February 2010.

Current Designation: Vice-Commissioner of Lhoka Prefecture since August 2013.

ZHANG YONGLIN

Year of Birth: June 1965

Ethnicity: Han Chinese

Year of Joining CCP: May 1984

Previous Designation: Party Secretary of Wanzhou Township of Chongqing Municipality from March 2010 to July 2013.

Current Designation: Vice-Commissioner of Lhoka Prefecture since July 2013.

Lhoka Prefecture PPCC

PEMPA

Year of Birth: July 1956 in Gongkar County of Lhoka

Ethnicity: Tibetan

Year of Joining CCP: January 1974

Previous Designation: Chairman of Lhoka PPCC and Standing Member of Lhoka Party Committee from January 2012 to September 2012.

Current Designation: Chairman of Lhoka PPCC since September 3, 2012.

Vice Chairmen of Lhoka PPCC

KHEDUP

Year of Birth: December 1957 Dranang County of Lhoka Prefecture

Ethnicity: Tibetan

Year of Joining CCP: December 1981

Previous Designation: Vice Chairman of Lhoka PPCC since August 1998

Current Designation: re-elected as Vice Chairman of Lhoka PPCC at the Tenth Lhoka PPCC's first meeting on September 3, 2012.

ZHANG SHIQING

Year of Birth: April 1956 in Lanzhou city of Gansu Province

Ethnicity: Han Chinese

Year of Joining CCP: November 1977

Previous Designation: Vice Chairman of Lhoka PPCC from September 2005-September 2012.

Current Designation: Re-elected as Vice Chairman of Lhoka PPCC at the Tenth Lhoka PPCC's first meeting on September3, 2012.

WANG HUAITING

Year of Birth: November 1956 in Shangqui County of Henan Province

Ethnicity: Han Chinese

Year of Joining CCP: May 1979

Previous Designation: Vice-Chairman of Lhoka PPCC from February 2008-September 2012.

Current Designation: Re-elected as Vice Chairman of Lhoka PPCC at the Tenth Lhoka PPCC's first meeting on September 3, 2012.

PHURBU DORJEE

Year of Birth: May 1963 in Gongkar County of Lhoka

Ethnicity: Tibetan

Education Qualification: a Graduate from Central Party School in Philosophy and Marxism.

Year of Joining CCP: May 1983

Previous Designation: Deputy Secretary General of Lhoka Party Committee from October 2007 to April 2012

Current Designation: Vice Chairman of Lhoka PPCC and Director of Lhoka Ethnic and Religious Affairs Bureau since September 3, 2012.

JAMYANG

Year of Birth: December 1959 in Nyedong County of Lhoka

Ethnicity: Tibetan

Year of Joining CCP: September 1978

Previous Designation: Deputy Director of Lhoka Organization Department, Deputy Minister of Human Resources and Social Security Bureau.

Current Designation: Vice Chairman of Lhoka PPCC since September 3, 2012.

PHURBU

Year of Birth: October 1962 in Lhodak County of Lhoka Prefecture

Ethnicity: Tibetan

Year of Joining CCP: July 1983

Previous Designation: Deputy Director of Lhoka Propaganda Department and Department of Cultural Affairs July 2010 –May 2012.

Current Designation: Vice Chairman of Lhoka PPCC since September 3, 2012.

SHENG ZHU

Year of Birth: January 1960 in Jiaonan of Shandong Province

Ethnicity: Han Chinese

Year of Joining CCP: August 1979

Previous Designation: Deputy Secretary of Lhoka Commission for Discipline Inspection and Director of Lhoka Supervision Bureau

Current Designation: Vice Chairman of Lhoka PPCC since September 3, 2012.

CHEN HAIQING

Year of Birth: September 1963 in Sichuan Province

Ethnicity: Han Chinese

Education Qualification: a graduate from Central Party School

Year of Joining CCP: November 1979

Previous Designation: Deputy Director of Lhoka Propaganda Department and Director of Regional Publicity Office, Lhoka Prefecture from September 2009-September 2012.

Current Designation: Vice Chairman of Lhoka PPCC since September 3, 2012.

NYIMA TASHI

Year of Birth: November 1965 in Dranang County of Lhoka Prefecture

Ethnicity: Tibetan

Year of Joining CCP: July 1988

Previous Designation: Governor and Deputy Secretary of Gongkar County, Lhoka Prefecture from December 2011-June 2013.

Current Designation: Vice-Chairman of Lhoka PPCC since June 2013.

CHAMDO (CH: CHANGDU/QAMDO) ADMINISTRATIVE DISTRICT (Changed to City in 2014)

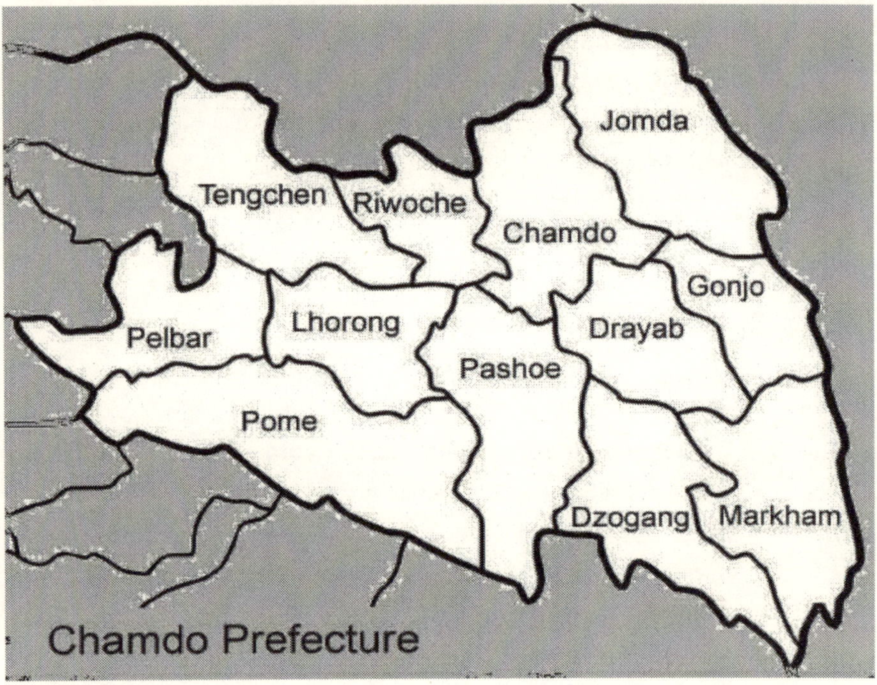

Chamdo/Qamdo AD is located in the eastern part of the Tibet Autonomous Region. The capital of the AD is Chamdo city. It covers an area of 108,600 sq. km. On its east is Sichuan, Yunnan to the south and Qinghai in the north. It administers 11 counties 13 districts 168 townships and 1,622 administrative villages. Its total population is over 657,505.

Chamdo Bangda Airport is the second highest airport in the world after Nagchu Dagring airport which is due to open for public use soon with an elevation of 4,334 metres (14,219 ft) and has the longest publicly used paved runway in the world, at 5.5 km (3 mi). It is also one of the most remote airports. The nearest city is Chamdo, which is two and a half hours away.

Counties under Chamdo AD:

Kharochu

Jomda

Gonjo

Riwoche

Tengchen

Drayab

Pashoe

Dzogang

Markham

Lhorong

Pelbar

Communist Party of Chamdo

ABHU
Secretary

Year of Birth: 1967 in Lhasa

Ethnicity: Muslim

Previous Designation: Vice Mayor of Lhasa Municipality People's Government from 2009-2012.

Current Designation: Deputy Secretary of Chamdo Party Committee and Vice-Commissioner of Chamdo Prefecture. Promoted as Party Secretary of Chamdo in 2016.

Vice Chairmen of Chamdo Party Committee

JAMYANG LODOE

Year of Birth: 1969 in Markham of Chamdo Prefecture

Ethnicity: Tibetan

Previous Designation: Vice-Commissioner of Chamdo Prefecture from 2009-2012.

Current Designation: Director of United Front Work Department (UFWD) of Chamdo and Standing Member of Chamdo Party Committee.

TENPA TASHI

Ethnicity: Tibetan

Previous Designation: Secretary General and Standing Member of Chamdo Party Committee.

Current Designation: Standing Member of Chamdo Party Committee and Vice-Commissioner of Chamdo.

RINCHEN YANGZOM

Ethnicity: Tibetan

Previous Designation: Vice Chairman of Chamdo People's Congress from 2010.

Current Designation: Deputy Director of Chamdo Propaganda Department and Standing Member of Chamdo Party Committee.

SANGAY TASHI

Ethnicity: Tibetan

Previous Designation: Vice-Chairman of Chamdo People's Congress.

Current Designation: Party Secretary of Markham County of Chamdo and Standing Member of Chamdo Party Committee.

XI TINGZANG

Year of Birth: 1963 in Luan County of Anhui Province.

Ethnicity: Han Chinese

Previous Designation: Deputy Secretary of Chamdo Party Committee and Vice-Commissioner of Chamdo Prefecture.

Current Designation: re-elected as Deputy Secretary of Chamdo Party Committee and Commissioner of Chamdo Prefecture in 2012.

TU TUNG KU

Ethnicity: Han Chinese

Previous Designation: Director of Organization Department of Chamdo and Standing Member of Chamdo Party Committee.

Current Designation: Deputy Secretary of Chamdo Party Committee and Director of Organization Department of Chamdo since 2012.

YAO HONG

Year of Birth: 1968 in Qijiang County of Chongqing Municipality.

Ethnicity: Tuijia

Previous Designation: Director of Propaganda Department of Chongqing Municipality and Standing Member of Chongqing Municipality from 2010-2012.

Current Designation: Deputy Secretary of Chamdo Party Committee from July 2013.

SHE XINGYU

Year of Birth: 1961

Ethnicity: Han Chinese

Previous Designation: Head of Chamdo Police Department from 2008 onwards.

Current Designation: Deputy Secretary of Chamdo Party Committee, Secretary of Chamdo Politics and Law Committee and Deputy Secretary of Chamdo Police Department.

XU DAOSHANG

Ethnicity: Han Chinese

Previous Designation: Deputy Secretary and Standing Member of Qin'an County.

Current Designation: Deputy Secretary of Chamdo Party Committee, Vice-Commissioner of Chamdo Prefecture and Tibet Aid Official since July 2013.

ZHANG KUNXI

Ethnicity: Han Chinese

Previous Designation: Deputy Chairman of Chamdo Politics and Law Committee from 2007 onwards.

Current Designation: Chairman of Chamdo Politics Committee and Standing Member of Chamdo Party Committee.

LIU FUKUNG

Ethnicity: Han Chinese

Previous Designation: Party Secretary of Shingtsa County of Nagchu Prefecture from 2010-2012.

Current Designation: Deputy Director of Organization Department of Chamdo and Standing Member of Chamdo Party Committee since 2013.

MA YIKU

Ethnicity: Han Chinese

Previous Designation: Judge of Chamdo People's Intermediate Court and Deputy Secretary of Chamdo Party Committee.

Current Designation: Secretary of Chamdo Discipline Committee and Standing Member of Chamdo Party Committee since July 2013.

DING WUNTANG

Ethnicity: Han Chinese

Previous Designation: Party Secretary of Pempa County of Chamdo Prefecture.

Current Designation: Standing Member of Chamdo Party Committee and Party Secretary of Bomda County of Chamdo Prefecture since 2013.

Chamdo Prefecture People's Congress

KUNCHOK GYALTSEN

Chairman

Ethnicity: Tibetan

Previous Designation: Director of Chamdo United Front Work Department (UFWD) and Standing Member of Chamdo Party Committee.

Current Designation: Chairman of Chamdo People's Congress from May 2012.

Vice-Chairman of Chamdo People's Congress

RINCHEN NORBU

Ethnicity: Tibetan

Previous Designation: Director and Deputy Secretary of Chamdo Advisory and Supervision Bureau.

Current Designation: Party Secretary of Markham County of Chamdo and Vice-Chairman of Chamdo People's Congress.

KUNGA TSERING

Ethnicity: Tibetan

Previous Designation: Deputy Secretary of Chamdo Party Committee and Governor of Chamdo District.

Current Designation: Vice-Chairman of Chamdo People's Congress since May 2012.

TSELO

Ethnicity: Tibetan

Previous Designation: Director of Chamdo Tourism Bureau

Current Designation: Vice-Chairman of Chamdo People's Congress since 2012.

TAO JINGUO

Ethnicity: Han Chinese

Previous Designation: Director and Deputy Secretary of Chamdo Advisory and Supervision Bureau

Current Designation: Vice Chairman of Chamdo People's Congress since 2013.

Chamdo Prefecture Administrative Commission

XI TINGZANG

Commissioner

Ethnicity: Han Chinese

(See page 140 for bio-details)

Vice-Commissioners

TENPA TASHI XU DAOSHANG

Tibetan Han Chinese

(See pages 140 and 141 respectively for the bio-details)

NYIMA DORJEE

Ethnicity: Tibetan

Previous Designation: Deputy Director of TAR Environment Department **Current Designation:** Vice-Commissioner of Chamdo Prefecture

LI SHIZHANG

Ethnicity: Han Chinese

Previous Designation: Governor and Deputy Secretary of Bomda (Ch: Jomda) county of Chamdo.

Current Designation: Vice-Commissioner of Chamdo Prefecture.

MA LITIAN

Ethnicity: Han Chinese

Previous Designation: Director of Chamdo Wealth and Political Committee

Current Designation: Vice-Commissioner of Chamdo Prefecture

QI DUANWU

Ethnicity: Han Chinese

Previous Designation: Party Secretary of Dali Autonomous Region of Yunnan Province.

Current Designation: Vice-Commissioner of Chamdo Prefecture since July 2013.

WANG WUI

Ethnicity: Han Chinese

Previous Designation: Secretary General of Chamdo Administrative Office from 2011 onwards.

Current Designation: Vice Commissioner of Chamdo Prefecture since 2013.

LI TIAN MING

Ethnicity: Han Chinese

Previous Designation: Governor and Deputy Secretary of Chamdo District.

Current Designation: Vice Commissioner of Chamdo Prefecture

LIU YUNDAI

Ethnicity: Han Chinese

Previous Designation: Director of TAR Tourism Bureau

Current Designation: Vice Commissioner of Chamdo Prefecture since 2013.

MI FENGJIAN

Year of Birth: 1977 in Hunan Province

Ethnicity: Han Chinese

Previous Designation: Governor and Deputy Secretary of Qingyuan District of Guangdong Province

Current Designation: Vice Commissioner of Chamdo Prefecture since July 2013.

SONAM DORJEE

Ethnicity: Tibetan

Previous Designation: Party Secretary of Pashoe County of Chamdo

Current Designation: Vice Commissioner of Chamdo Prefecture since 2011.

People's Political Consultative Conference of Chamdo Prefecture

WANGDUE

Year of Birth: 1962 in Rutog County of Ngari Prefecture

Ethnicity: Tibetan

Previous Designation: Deputy Secretary of Chamdo Party Committee and Secretary of Chamdo Politics and Law Committee from 2008 onwards.

Current Designation: Chairman of Chamdo PPCC.

Vice Chairmen of Chamdo PPCC

JUNGLO JAMPA KHEDUP

Ethnicity: Tibetan

(See Page 44 for bio-details)

TASHI PALMO *(f)*

Ethnicity: Tibetan

Current Designation: Vice Chairman of Chamdo PPCC

THUPGA

Year of Birth: 1955 in Chamdo

Ethnicity: Tibetan

Previous Designation: Director of Chamdo Cultural Relic Bureau.

Current Designation: Vice Commissioner of Chamdo Prefecture.

DAMCHOE RINCHEN JUNYE

Ethnicity: Tibetan Tulku

Current Designation: Vice Commissioner of Chamdo Prefecture.

TRINLAY

Ethnicity: Tibetan

Previous Designation: Party Secretary of Lhorong County of Chamdo Prefecture.

Current Designation: Party Secretary of Lhorong County of Chamdo Prefecture and Vice-Commissioner of Chamdo Prefecture since December 2012.

LI KUNDU

Ethnicity: Han Chinese

Previous Designation: Director of Chamdo Tourism Bureau.

Current Designation: Vice-Commissioner of Chamdo.

YANG KEYUAN

Ethnicity: Han Chinese

Previous Designation: Director of Development and Reform Commission of Chamdo Prefecture.

Current Designation: Vice Commissioner of Chamdo Prefecture since December 2012.

GAO ZHONGHUI

Ethnicity: Han Chinese

Previous Designation: Director of Land and Resource Department of Chamdo Prefecture.

Current Designation: Vice-Commissioner of Chamdo Prefecture.

JIN SHIHUN

Ethnicity: Han Chinese

Previous Designation: Party Secretary of Drayab County of Chamdo Prefecture.

Current Designation: Vice Commissioner of Chamdo Prefecture.

YANG JIANPIN

Ethnicity: Han Chinese

Previous Designation: Deputy Director of United Front Work Department (UFWD) of Chamdo Prefecture.

Current Designation: Vice Commissioner of Chamdo Prefecture.

MISC

NORBU DHONDUP

Ethnicity: Tibetan

Year of Birth: 1960

Joined CCP in 1978 as stated working for CCP in August 1978.

Misc/Current: He is the seniormost Party official in TAR at this level. In March 2019 at a meeting on social stability, Norbu Dhondup said it is "imperative to knock down those who lead others to fly....and target those who come to be self-immolation, terrorists and extremists; destroy legal organisations; and highlight the dignity of our legal and socialist system. We should start to use every power. A hunting dog's sense of smell, ecstatic sense of wearing as a falcons ability to see, so that we can fight strongly in intelligence and the interest to know (the enemy) before they take any action". The strong statement could have been made also brighten his chances of elevation to the CCP CC.

Graduated from Central Party School.

(See Page 33 for bio-details)

NYINGTRI/NYINGCHI (CH: LINZHI) ADMINISTRATIVE DISTRICT

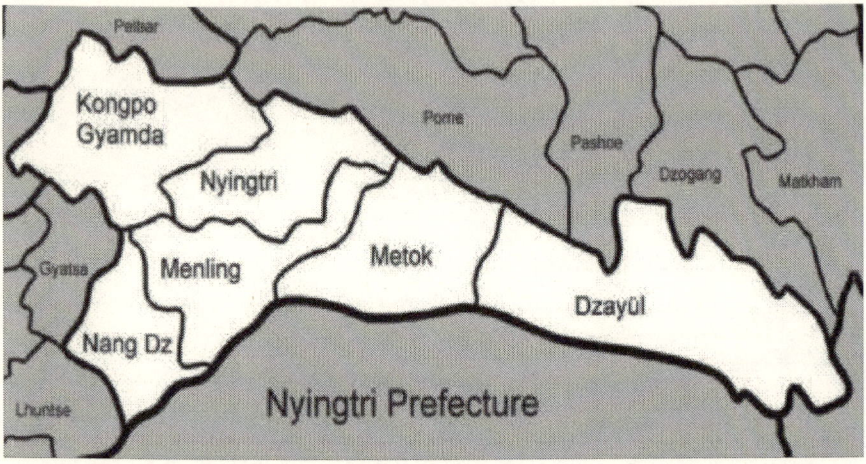

Linzhi/Nyingchi AD borders Arunachal Pradesh and is surrounded by Lhasa and Shannan (Lhoka), Naqu (Nagchu) and Changdu (Chamdo) ADs in the west, north and east. Bayi Town (Tib: Dayib), is the administrative headquarters of Linzhi, located 406 km east of Lhasa, and is also a PLA missile base.

It contains the Namcha Barwa Peak and the Yarlung Tsangpo Great Canyon located in Medog County, which are significant for geoscientific studies and tourism. Approximately 90 km west of Gongbo'gyamda County is the alpine Basum Lake at about 3,538 metres above sea level, covering an area of 25.9 sq. km. Its surroundings are populated by diverse wildlife including leopards, bears, goats and musk deer. The lake contains an inlet with a Gelug monastery. East of Linzhi County is the Seche La Mountain, a mountain of the Nyenchen Tanglha Mountain Range, which forms part of the watershed of the Nyang River and the Polung Zangbo River. Benri La Mountain, near the small town of Dagze, is a sacred site of the Tibetan Bon Sect.

Nyingtri airport was opened for traffic on March 20, 2006. A new automated navigation system was inaugurated in September 2006 to guide in the first commercial flight.

Nyingchi Airport was the third airport that Tibet put into operation. Built at a cost of 780 million yuan (US$ 96.18 million), including investment by the General Administration of Civil Aviation of China (CAAC), the airport is 2,949 meters above sea level, lower than the other two civil airports, with a designed annual passenger flow of 120,000.

(**Note**: Official Chinese maps depict almost the entire Indian state of Arunachal Pradesh within the geographic boundaries of Nyingtri/Nyingchi Prefecture.)

Counties under Nyingtri AD:

Nyingtri

Kongpo Gyamda

Menling

Metok

Bome

Dzayul

Nang

Communist Party of Nyingtri Prefecture

ZHAO SHIJUN

Party Secretary

Year of Birth: 1958 in Zhuzhou County of Hunan Province.

Ethnicity: Han Chinese

Previous Designation: Deputy Director TAR Tourism Bureau and Deputy Secretary of TAR Party Committee from 2004-2012, Party Secretary of Nyingtri Prefecture and Vice Commissioner of Nyingtri Prefecture.

Current Designation: Party Secretary of Nyingtri Prefecture since 2012.

Deputy Secretaries of Nyingtri Party Committee

DORJEE TSERING

Ethnicity: Tibetan

Previous Designation: Vice Commissioner of Nyingtri Prefecture.

Current Designation: Deputy Secretary of Nyingtri Party Committee, Secretary of Nyingtri Politics and Law Committee and Secretary of Nyingtri Police Department.

DAWA NGODUP

Ethnicity: Tibetan

Previous Designation: Standing Member of Lhasa Municipal Party Committee and Secretary of Discipline Inspection Committee of Lhasa from 2009-2012.

Current Designation: Vice Chairman of Nyingtri Party Committee and Director of Nyingtri Organization Department since 2012.

NGAWANG

Year of Birth: 1966

Ethnicity: Tibetan

Previous Designation: Official of Nyingtri Political Committee Branch

Current Designation: Standing Member of Nyingtri Prefecture Party Committee and Official of Political Committee Nyingtri Branch since 2012.

PHUNTSOK DORJEE

Ethnicity: Tibetan

Previous Designation: Vice Commissioner of Nyingtri Prefecture from 2005-2011.

Current Designation: Standing Member of Nyingtri Party Committee and Director of Nyingtri United Front Work Department (UFWD) since 2011.

YUNKYI

Ethnicity: Tibetan

Previous Designation: Deputy Director of TAR Development and Reform Commission

Current Designation: Standing Member of Nyingtri Party Committee and Vice-Commissioner of Nyingtri Prefecture since end of 2012.

WANGDUE

Ethnicity: Tibetan

Previous Designation: Vice Commissioner of Shigatse Prefecture and Standing Member of Shigatse Party Committee from 2011 to 2013.

Current Designation: Deputy Secretary of Nyingtri Party Committee and Commissioner of Nyingtri Prefecture since July 2013.

LI HAIBO

Ethnicity: Han Chinese

Previous Designation: Secretary General of Ningde County of Fujian Province and Standing Member of Fujian Party Committee and Director of Fujian United Front Work Department (UFWD) from 2011 to 2013.

Current Designation: Deputy Secretary of Nyingtri Party Committee, Vice Commissioner of Nyingtri Prefecture and Tibet Aid Official since July 2013.

CAI ZHAHA

Year of Birth: 1966 in Guangdong Province

Ethnicity: Han Chinese

Previous Designation: Party Secretary of Gompo Gyamda County from 2010 to 2013.

Current Designation: Deputy Secretary of Nyingtri Party Committee, Vice Commissioner of Nyingtri Prefecture and Tibet Aid Official since July 2013.

BU BUI

Ethnicity: Han Chinese

Previous Designation: Deputy Secretary General of Nyingtri TAR Party Committee from 2006 onwards.

Current Designation: Standing Member of Nyingtri Party Committee and Secretary of Nyingtri Discipline Inspection Committee.

HONG BUI

Year of Birth: 1965 in Tsada County of Ngari Prefecture.

Ethnicity: Tibetan

Previous Designation: Vice Commissioner of Nyingtri Prefecture

Current Designation: Standing Member of Nyingtri Party Committee and Vice Commissioner of Nyingtri Prefecture since 2012.

XIAN YAN *(f)*

Year of Birth: 1973

Ethnicity: Han Chinese

Previous Designation: Deputy Director of TAR Press and Publication Bureau

Current Designation: Standing Member of Nyingtri Party Committee and Director of Nyingtri Propaganda Department since December 2012.

TAO HUIMING

Year of Birth: 1955 in Hunan Province

Ethnicity: Han Chinese

Previous Designation: Vice Commissioner of Nyingtri Prefecture from 2008 onwards.

Current Designation: Standing Member of Nyingtri Party Committee and Vice Commissioner of Nyingtri Prefecture since 2012.

Nyingtri Prefecture People's Congress

LI LAIXIN

Chairman

Ethnicity: Han Chinese

Previous Designation: Standing Member of Nyingtri Party Committee and Vice Commissioner of Nyingtri Prefecture from 2011-2012.

Current Designation: Chairman of Nyingtri People's Congress since 2013.

Vice Chairman of Nyingtri People's Congress

TSEWANG JIGME

Ethnicity: Tibetan

Previous Designation: Secretary and Director of Nyingtri Forestry Department from 2011 onwards.

Current Designation: Vice Chairman of Nyingtri People's Congress since 2011.

LAN ZHENHA

Year of Birth: 1955

Ethnicity: Han Chinese

Previous Designation: Director of Nyingtri Land and Resource Department from 2002 to 2008.

Current Designation: Vice-Chairman of Nyingtri People's Congress since 2008.

DORJEE

Ethnicity: Tibetan

Current Designation: Vice-Chairman of Nyingtri People's Congress.

Nyingtri Prefectural Administrative Commission

WANGDUE

Chief Commissioner

Ethnicity: Tibetan

(See Page 153 for bio-details)

Vice-Commissioners

LI HEIBAO

Ethnicity: Han Chinese

CAI ZHAHA

Han Chinese

HONG BUI

Han Chinese

(See page 153 and 154 for their bio-details)

TAO HUIMING

Han Chinese

(See page 154 for his bio-details)

DAWA

Ethnicity: Tibetan

Previous Designation: Secretary of Nyingtri State Revenue Department.

Current Designation: Vice- Commissioner of Nyingtri Prefecture since 2011.

PASANG

Ethnicity: Tibetan

Current Designation: Vice Commissioner of Nyingtri Prefecture since 2011.

DHONKYI

Ethnicity: Tibetan

Current Designation: Vice-Commissioner of Nyingtri Prefecture since 2007.

LI SANG *(f)*

Ethnicity: Tibetan

Previous Designation: Governor and Party Secretary of Gompo Gyamda County.

Current Designation: Vice Commissioner of Nyingtri Prefecture since December 2012.

YANG FANGYI

Ethnicity: Han Chinese

Current Designation: Vice Commissioner of Nyingtri Prefecture since 2007.

MUI ZHAKU

Ethnicity: Han Chinese

Previous Designation: Director of Nyingtri Development and Reform Commission.

Current Designation: Vice Commissioner of Nyingtri Prefecture since 2012.

HE YIHUI

Ethnicity: Han Chinese

Previous Designation: Party Secretary of Sizadegu County of Ngawa (Ch: Aba) Autonomous Prefecture from 2011 to 2013

Current Designation: Vice Commissioner of Nyingtri Prefecture since July 2013.

ZHANG KONGYAN

Ethnicity: Han Chinese

Current Designation: Vice Commissioner of Nyingtri Prefecture since 2012.

People's Political Consultative Conference of Nyingtri Prefecture

SANGAY DAKPAN

Chairman

Ethnicity: Menpa from Metok County of Nyingtri Prefecture

Previous Designation: Deputy Secretary and Director of TAR Forestry Department from 2006 to 2009.

Current Designation: Chairman of Nyingtri PPCC since 2009.

Vice Chairmen of Nyingtri PPCC

TENPAY NYIMA

Year of Birth: 1943 in Gompo Gyamda

Ethnicity: Tibetan Tulku from Lhalung Monastery of Nyingtri Prefecture.

Current Designation: Member of TAR Buddhist Association and Vice Chairman of Nyingtri PPCC.

KARMA

Ethnicity: Tibetan

Current Designation: Vice Chairman of Nyingtri PPCC.

PHURBU DORJEE

Ethnicity: Tibetan

Current Designation: Vice Chairman of Nyingtri PPCC and Deputy Director of Nyingtri Organization Department.

LOBSANG

Ethnicity: Tibetan

Current Designation: Vice Chairman of Nyingri PPCC.

DING BULAI

Year of Birth: 1963 in Beijing

Ethnicity: Han Chinese

Previous Designation: Deputy Director of TAR Animal Husbandry Department.

Current Designation: Vice Chairman of Nyingtri PPCC.

DING SONGSHANG

Ethnicity: Han Chinese

Previous Designation: Director of Nyingtri Pastoral Development Office.

Current Designation: Vice Chairman of Nyingtri PPCC.

SHAI GONGMIN

Ethnicity: Han Chinese

Previous Designation: Secretary of Nyingtri Development and Reform Commission from 2006 onwards.

Current Designation: Vice Chairman of Nyingtri PPCC.

LI LANPING *(f)*

Ethnicity: Han Chinese

Previous Designation: Secretary and Director of Nyingtri Tourism Department.

Current Designation: Vice Chairman of Nyingtri PPCC.

HU YIDING

Ethnicity: Tibetan

Current Designation: Vice Chairman of Nyingtri PPCC.

NAQU (NAGCHU) ADMINISTRATIVE DISTRICT

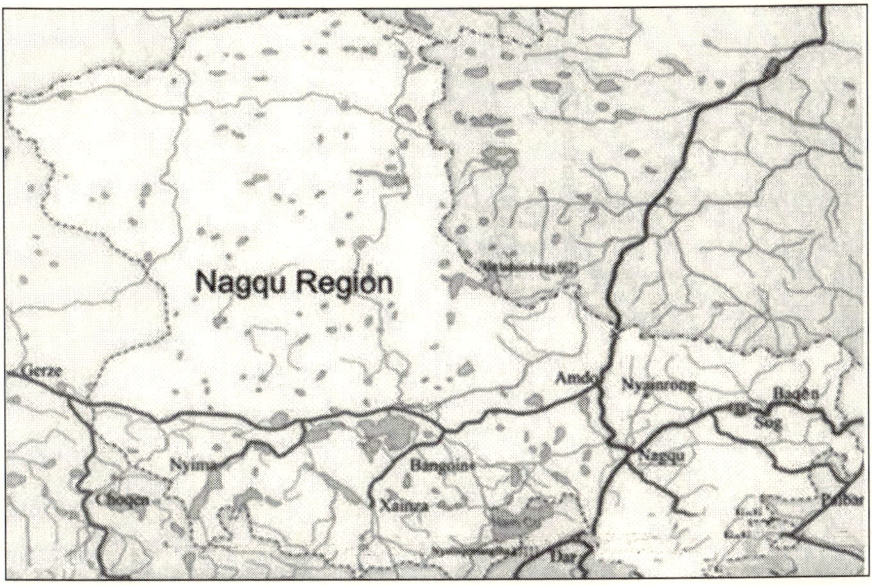

Nagqu/Nagchu Administrative District lies in the northern part of TAR. It borders Chamdo in the east, Ngari in the west, Lhasa, Nyingtri and Shigatse in the south and the Xinjiang-Uighur Autonomous Region and Qinghai Province in the north. It is surrounded by the Tanggula, Nyainqentanglha, Kangdese and the snow-capped Dargo Mountains in the west and the Burgyi Mountain in the east. Nagchu town is a political, economic, cultural and trading centre. Connected by the Xining-Lhasa, Nagchu-Chamdo and Amdo-Shiquanhe (Tib: Tsonye) Highways, Nagchu town is a transport-hub connecting TAR and China. All counties and townships within Nagchu AD are accessible by highways. The population of Nagchu AD is 462,382. It exercises jurisdiction over 10 counties and the Shuanghu Special Administrative Zone, which comprises 145 townships.

Since September 2007, the authorities have been building TAR's biggest logistics centre in Nagchu Township. The centre covers an area of 533 hectares and is located next to Nagchu railway station at an altitude of 4,500 metres.

China begun to construct Nagchu Dagring Airport in 2011 with an investment of 1.8 billion Yuan (US$ 263 million) and covers 233 to 266 hectares. The airport was supposed to be completed in 2015, but is not open yet. It will be the highest airport in the world at 4,436 m (14,554 ft), surpassing Chamdo Bangda Airport as the highest. The airport is part of a Chinese government development scheme to build 97 additional airports across China by 2020. By then, the authorities intend that four-fifths of China's population will be within a 90-minute drive of an airport.

Counties under Nagchu Administrative District

Nagchu

Lhari

Driru

Nyainrong

Amdo

Xainza

Sog

Bangoin

Dachen

Nyima

Tsonye

Communist Party of Nagchu (Ch: Nagqu) Prefecture

SANGAY TASHI

Party Secretary of Nagchu Party Committee and Administrative Commissioner of Nagchu

Ethnicity: Tibetan

Previous Designation: Party Deputy Secretary of Nagchu Party Committee and Administrative Commissioner of Nagchu. Party Secretary of Markham County of Chamdo and Standing Member of Chamdo Party Committee. Vice Chairman of Nagchu Party Committee and Party Secretary of Sog County of Nagchu since July 2013.

Deputy Secretaries of Nagchu Party Committee

SONAM DAKPA

Ethnicity: Tibetan

Previous Designation: Party Secretary of Palgong County of Ngachu Prefecture, Standing Member of Ngachu Party Committee and Director of Ngachu Organization Department.

Current Designation: Vice Chairman of Nagchu Party Committee and Director of Nagchu Organization Department since July 2013.

TSERING NAMGON

Ethnicity: Tibetan

Previous Designation: Deputy Secretary and Governor of Driru County, Nagchu Prefecture.

Current Designation: Chairman of United Front Work Department of Nagchu Prefecture since 2011.

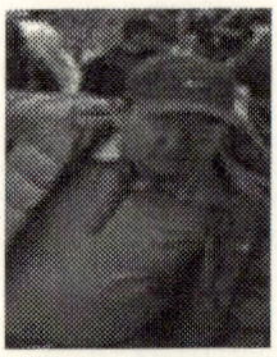

SONAM GAWA

Ethnicity: Tibetan

Current Designation: Party Secretary of Lhari County of Nagchu Prefecture and Standing Member of Nagchu Party Committee since 2013.

DORJEE GYALTSEN

Ethnicity: Tibetan

Previous Designation: Governor of Dachen and Palgon County of Nagchu.

Current Designation: Head of Nagchu Propaganda Department and Standing Member of Nagchu Party Committee since 2008.

GONGHUI CAI

Year of Birth: 1968 in Sichuan Province.

Ethnicity: Han Chinese

Previous Designation: Mayor of Lhasa Municipality, Standing Member of Lhasa Municipality and Head of Local Public Security Bureau.

Current Designation: Secretary of Prefectural Politics and Law Committee, Head of Local Public Security Department and Vice Chairman of Nagchu Party Committee since May 2013.

LI HUA

Year of Birth: 1965 in Zhejiang Province

Ethnicity: Han Chinese

Previous Designation: Party Secretaty of Zhoushan County of Zhejiang Province and Standing Member of Quzhou City Party Committee from 2011-2013.

Current Designation: Vice Commissioner of Nagchu Prefecture, Standing Member of Nagchu Party Committee and Tibet Aid Official since July 2013.

WANG YADONG

Year of Birth: 1961

Ethnicity: Han Chinese

Previous Designation: Deputy Secretary General of Nagchu Prefecture Party Committee.

Current Designation: Secretary General and Standing Member of Nagchu Party Committee since July 2013.

OU LIJIN

Ethnicity: Han Chinese

Previous Designation: Vice Commissioner of Chamdo Prefecture.

Current Designation: Vice Commissioner of Nagchu Prefecture and Standing Member of Nagchu Party Committee since 2012.

HU LIN

Ethnicity: Han Chinese

Previous Designation: Party Secretary of Nyarong County, Nagchu Prefecture.

Current Designation: Secretary of Nagchu Discipline Committee and Standing Member of Ngachu Party Committee since 2012.

Nagchu/Naqu Prefecture People's Congress

TAO HONG YANG

Chairman

Ethnicity: Han Chinese

Previous Designation: Party Secretary of Gompa County, Standing Member of Nagchu Party Committee, Secretary General of Nagchu Party Committee, Secretary of Nagchu Politics and Law Committee and Deputy Secretary of Secretary of Nagchu Party Committee since 2012.

Current Designation: Chairman of Nagchu People's Congress.

Vice Chairman of Nagchu People's Congress

JAMYANG DORJEE

Ethnicity: Tibetan

Current Designation: Vice Chairman of Nagchu People's Congress.

TRINLAY KHEDUP

Ethnicity: Tibetan

PreviousDesignation: Inspector of Nagchu Branch of TAR Commission for Discipline Inspection from January 2013.

Current Designation: Vice Chairman of Nagchu People's Congress since July 2013.

WEISHI KUI

Year of Birth: 1962 in Shanxi Province

Ethnicity: Han

Previous Designation: Party Secretary of Shingtsa County, Ngachu Prefecture.

Current Designation: Vice Chairman of Nagchu People's Congress since 2009.

Nagchu Prefecture Administrative Commission

GAO YANG

Former Party Secretary

Year of Birth: October 1957

Ethnicity: Han Chinese

Year of Joining CCP: August 1983

Education: Post graduation in Meteorological Communication from Chengdu School of Meteorology.

Vice Commissioners

KELSANG MONLAM

Year of Birth: 1970 in Kham Phayul

Ethnicity: Tibetan

Previous Designation: Governor and Deputy Secretary of Sog County, Nagchu Prefecture from 2009-2011.

Current Designation: Vice Commissioner of Nagchu Prefecture since 2012.

OGA

Ethnicity: Tibetan

Previous Designation: Director of Nagchu Housing and Infrastructure Development Office.

Current Designation: Vice Commissioner of Nagchu Prefecture.

TAGYAM

Ethnicity: Tibetan

Current Designation: Vice Commissioner of Nagchu Prefecture.

PHUDON *(f)*

Ethnicity: Tibetan from Nagchu Prefecture.

Previous Designation: Official of Nagchu Resource and Politics Committee in 1988.

Current Designation: Vice Commissioner of Nagchu Prefecture and Director of Nagchu Resource and Politics Committee.

DORJEE RABTEN

Ethnicity: Tibetan

Previous Designation: Deputy Secretary of Nagchu Party Committee and Director of Nagchu Land and Pastoral Committee from 2009 onwards.

Current Designation: Vice Commissioner of Nagchu Prefecture.

DICKYI DOLKAR *(f)*

Ethnicity: Tibetan

Previous Designation: Governor, Party Secretary and Deputy Secretary of Nyarong County of Nagchu Prefecture.

Current Designation: Vice Commissioner of Nagchu Prefecture from August 2013.

Li Hua

Ethnicity: Han Chinese

Ou Lijin

Han Chinese

(See Page 164 and 165 for their bio-details)

CAO YONGSHOU

Year of Birth: 1967 from Tsongon of Amdo

Ethnicity: Tibetan

Previous Designation: Governor and Deputy Secretary of Nangchen County of Tsongon, Amdo from 2011-2013.

Current Designation: Party Secretary of Nyarong County and Vice Commissioner of Nagchu Prefecture since August 2013.

PAO DUNG

Year of Birth: 1966 in Zhejiang Province

Ethnicity: Han Chinese

Previous Designation: Deputy Director of Water Bueau of Trinkuchu (CH: Chengguan) Township of Lhasa.

Current Designation: Vice Commissioner of Nagchu Prefecture since July 2013.

ZHANG JUN

Ethnicity: Han Chinese

Current Designation: Vice Commissioner of Nagchu Prefecture.

People's Political Consultative Conference of Nagchu Prefecture

GYALTSEN WANGDAK

Chairman

Ethnicity: Tibetan from Nagchu Prefecture.

Previous Designation: Party Secretary of Nagchu Land and Pastoral Bureau, Vice Commissioner of Nagchu Prefecture from 2006-2012.

Current Designation: Chairman of PPCC Nagchu Prefecture since 2012.

Vice Chairman of Nagchu PPCC

SONAM GYALTSEN

Ethnicity: Tibetan from Nagchu Prefecture.

Current Designation: Vice Commissioner of Nagchu Prefecture and Vice Chairman of TAR PPCC.

LHODAK

Ethnicity: Tibetan

Current Designation: Deputy Secretary of Nagchu Party Committee and Vice Chairman of Nagchu PPCC.

YON DAKPA

Year of Birth: 1962 in Sog County of Nagchu Prefecture.

Ethnicity: Tibetan

Previous Designation: Governor of Driru County of Nagchu Prefecture from 2001 onwards.

Current Designation: Vice Chairman of PPCC Nagchu Prefecture and Director of Regional Advisory and Exercise Committee.

KUNGA RINCHEN

Ethnicity: Tibetan

Current Designation: Vice Chairman of PPCC, Nagchu Prefecture.

SONAM

Ethnicity: Tibetan

Previous Designation: Deputy Secretary of Nagchu Party Committee.

Current Designation: Chairman of Nagchu Propaganda Department and Vice Chairman of PPCC, Nagchu Prefecture.

TANAM

Ethnicity: Tibetan

Previous Designation: Governor of Palgon County of Nagchu and Deputy Secretary of Nagchu Party Committee.

Current Designation: Vice Chairman of PPCC, Nagchu Prefecture.

JI GONGMIN

Ethnicity: Han Chinese

Previous Designation: Deputy Secretary of Ngachu Politics and Law Committee.

Current Designation: Vice Chairman of PPCC, Nagchu Prefecture.

LI TELIN

Ethnicity: Han Chinese

Previous Designation: Director of Human resources and Social Security Department of Nagchu.

Current Designation: Vice Chairman of PPCC, Nagchu Prefecture.

APPENDIX-I

CHINESE LEADERS INFLUENTIAL ON TIBET POLICY

This list identifies 36 Chinese Communist Party (CCP) leaders who have had a direct policy and/or operational experience in the Tibet Autonomous Region (TAR) or its adjoining Tibetan regions. They are assessed as wielding adequate influence to amend, slow down and, in some circumstances possibly even completely scuttle, proposals concerning Tibet that may be mooted by senior levels in the incumbent CCP leadership. They comprise cadres who have recently retired from senior leadership positions or are still serving. Significantly, and reflecting Tibet's importance to China's leadership, their numbers are possibly higher than for any other province in China except the capital, Beijing.

The 36 are: (i) Ma Kai; (ii) Wang Zhaoguo; (iii) Wang Huning; (iv) Legchok; (v) Zhu Weiqun; (vi) Jampa Phuntsog; (vii) Liu Yandong; (viii) Liu Qibao; (ix) Du Qinglin; (x) Li Keqiang; (xi) Yang Chuantang; (xii) Zhang Ping; (xiii) Zhang Qingli; (xiv) Chen Kuiyuan; (xv) Meng Jianzhu; (xvi) Zhao Leji; (xvii) Hu Chunhua; (xviii) Hu Jintao; (xix) Qin Guangrong; (xx) Yuan Chunqing; (xxi) Geng Huichang; (xxii) Nie Weiguo, (xxiii) Jia Qinglin; (xxiv) Guo Jinlong; (xxv) Dong Guishan; (xxvi) Jiang Jufeng; (xxvii) Qiang Wei; (xxviii) Danke; (xxix) Yang Song; (xxx) Zhang Yijiong; (xxxi) Dorjee; (xxxii) Ye Xiaowen; (xxxiii) Li Chongxi; (xxxiv) Yang Huanning; (xxxv) Chen Quanguo; and (xxxvi) Li Zhanshu.

[(Note: **Zhou Yongkang**, a former PBSC Member is not included in this list consequent to his expulsion from the CCP and sentencing to life imprisonment without political rights.

Ling Jihua is not included following his demotion as member of the 18th CCP CC and subsequent abrupt removal in December 2014 as Head of the Party's United Front Work Department and dismissed from the CCP. Ling Jihua has, however, long been close to the officials of the TAR, especially during the periods of Zhang Qingli and Chen Quanguo. In recent years he was regularly co-opted into the TAR's annual NPC and CPPCC delegations in acknowledgement of the work he has done on Tibet's behalf.

Lt. General Yang Jinshan is also not included as he was dismissed in 2014 on charges of corruption. Lt General Yang Jinshan was a PLA Deputy Commander of the Tibet Military Region and one of the senior PLA officers who accompanied Chinese Defense Minister Liang Guanglie to Sri Lanka and India.

General Wang Jianping: General Wang Jianping has been Commander of China's People's Armed Police since 2009. He was promoted to the rank of General in December 2012. He was arrested on charges of corruption on August 25, 2016, becoming the first serving PLA General to be arrested.

Between 1996 and 2000 while Chen Kuiyuan was Party Secretary and Guo Jinlong as well as Yang Chuantang were Deputy Secretaries of TAR, Wang Jianping commanded the PAP Headquarters in Tibet and was closely associated with policies in Tibet.

General Tian Xiusi: General Tian Xiusi was till recently Political Commissar of the PLA Chengdu Military Region and Political Commissar of the PLA Air Force; he was one of three senior military officers with experience of West China to be promoted to General in July 2012. He is a member of the 18th CCP CC. In July 2016, however, reports surfaced of his being investigated for corruption. If sentenced, he will have no say in policy matters.

Tian Xiusi began his military career in the Xinjiang Military District in 1968 and rose to become the Political Commissar of the Xinjiang Military District. At the end of 2009 – in the wake of the 2008 Lhasa unrest and Tibetan demonstrations in Sichuan -- he was transferred out of Xinjiang (in a move reminiscent of Zhang Qingli's 2006 transfer to Tibet) and made Political Commissar of the Chengdu Military Region where his role in Tibet affairs has been an obvious priority. At the end of October Tian Xiusi was promoted and moved to the Center as Political Commissar of the PLA Air Force. As the PLA Air Force devotes greater attention and resources to Southwest China and the India border, Tian Xiusi was well-placed to have a voice on Tibet security issues.)]

Hu Jintao: Despite his retirement at the 18th Party Congress in 2012, Hu Jintao will continue to retain interest in how the Tibet problem is handled under his successor's direction. Because of his close relationship with Chinese President Xi Jinping and out of respect for his service to the Party as General Secretary and as Party Secretary in Tibet, he is likely to be consulted on all new ideas and planning. His approval can be anticipated to be a key factor in formulating and unveiling any future policy shifts on Tibet.

Li Keqiang: While Li Keqiang's involvement in Tibet matters has earlier been negligible, as Premier he will be involved in drafting and approving policies for the TAR and adjoining Tibetan regions. Chen Quanguo, till recently TAR Party Secretary, and Li Keqiang also have a long history of working together shoulder-to-shoulder in Henan and Hebei.

Wang Huning: Wang Huning has maintained a close relationship with Tibet in recent years as visible from his being listed as a member of all TAR delegations to the NPC and the CPPCC. In fact, Wang Huning's name heads the TAR name list of delegates to the 18th Party Congress. Wang Huning was very close to Hu Jintao and continues to be very influential under Xi Jinping. He is a Member of the Politburo, heads the CCP's secretive Central Policy Research Office and is a member of the CCP CC Secretariat that has been reconstituted by Xi Jinping. His finger prints are all over the present policies in Tibet and any changes in Tibet policy will certainly be routed through his office.

Li Zhanshu: Born into a revolutionary communist family in Pingshan County in Hebei Province, Li Zhanshu is a 'second-generation Red'. After Ling Jihua's demotion, he was appointed Director of the Central Committee's pivotal General Office, which is directly under the CCP CC General Secretary. He also took over as Party Secretary of the 'Work Committee overseeing All Party Organizations Operating Directly Under Party Central in Beijing'. He is consequently Xi Jinping's private secretary. Li Zhanshu rose rapidly during the Hu Jintao decade. His early career was in the Communist Youth League (CYL) and he later served many years in Shaanxi (Xi Jinping's home province), and was also Party Secretary in Heilongjiang (sensitive border issues with a foreign country) and Guizhou (minority nationality issues).

Li Zhanshu's friendship with Xi Jinping began about three decades ago, when Xi Jinping served as Deputy Party Secretary and then Party Secretary of

Zhengding county in Hebei from 1982 to 1985 and Li Zhanshu served as Party Secretary of the neighbouring Wuji county in the same province from 1983 to 1985. Both counties belong to Shijiazhuang prefecture. Li Zhanshu later spent five years in Shaanxi serving as Director of the Organization Department of the provincial party committee, Party Secretary of Xi'an and Deputy Party Secretary of Shaanxi Province. This background and work experience were factors in Xi Jinping appointing him Chief of Staff. Li Zhanshu has worked closely with Xi Jinping and will certainly help Xi Jinping in shaping issues on Tibet. He is a member of the Politburo.

Zhang Dejiang: is a 'princeling', member of the PBSC and Chairman of the Chinese People's Political Consultative Conference (CPPCC), which supervises matters relating to China's ethnic minorities and non-CCP entities. He is also Chairman of the Central Committee Tibet Work Coordination Small Group. His opinions on Tibet have so far favoured continuing the earlier approach and been no different from those of persons like Wu Bangguo or Jia Qinglin.

Liu Yandong *(f)*: A member of the 18th Politburo and daughter of Liu Ruilong, Mao Zedong's Vice Minister of Agriculture, Liu Yandong is a 'princeling' and the fifth woman to have risen to such heights in the CCP. She has been Director of the CCP CC's UFWD and was familiar with the Tibet issue, though she was never reported to have taken special interest in the subject. Though Tibet does not appear to be part of her brief as a member of the Politburo, her experience is likely to be used. Hu Jintao has been her mentor.

Liu Yunshan: Liu Yunshan is an important member of the PBSC and has a place in the CCP CC Secretariat constituted by Xi Jinping. He is the Party's Propaganda 'Supremo' and continues to oversee the Party's propaganda portfolio. After some early experience in the CYL, he was spotted for promotion to the Centre after 11 years of working experience in Inner Mongolia. His rise, however, came under Hu Jintao. During the riots in Tibet in 2008 , he played an important role in ensuring that the propaganda apparatus for the first time effectively turned the majority Han population against the Tibetans. He has orthodox political views and he is likely to advocate a cautious and conservative policy on Tibet.

Wang Zhaoguo: Wang Zhaoguo was a protégée of Zhao Ziyang and headed the CCP CC's United Front Work Department for a decade during the Jiang Zemin years. His personal focus was on Taiwan affairs, but he did follow matters relating to Tibet. Credible reports indicate that Jiang Zemin did not find him insightful on Tibet matters and preferred to consult other advisors. Wang Zhaoguo was elevated to the Politburo in 2003.

Du Qinglin: A protégé of Hu Jintao, Du Qinglin is a Vice Chairman of the CPPCC and member of the 18th CCP CC. Interestingly, Xi Jinping appointed him a member of the powerful 18th CCP CC Secretariat though he was past the retirement age. Du Qinglin was head of the UFWD from 2007-2012. His appointments indicate he will play a role on matters related to Tibet.

Zhu Weiqun: Zhu Weiqun is presently Chairman of the Ethnic and Religious Affairs Committee of the National People's Congress (NPC) and is fairly active and strident on issues concerning Tibet. His remarks regarding the Dalai Lama, made during NPC sessions in March 2014 and 2016 and on other occasions including on the issue of the Dalai Lama's reincarnation,were widely reported and uncontested. He has extensive knowledge regarding Tibet and Buddhism and his views are orthodox and conservative. He will wield considerable influence on matters regarding Tibet and Buddhism.

The extent of his influence was suggested when after Zhang Yijiong replaced him as Executive Vice Minister of the United Front Department and as China's representative in any possible future talks with the Dalai Lama's representatives in June 2012, Zhu Weiqun did not immediately step aside. He remained as the No.2 ranked Vice Minister (accorded full Minister rank) in the UFWD with Zhang Yijiong ranked at No.3 below him. Zhu Weiqun also acted as the chief personal escort of Standing Committee member Li Changchun during his much publicized trip to Tibet that August and followed that up with an anniversary commemoration visit to Labrang Monastery in Gansu. During the visit the official Chinese media identified Zhu Weiqun by a title he has held for years but has been seldom used previously i.e. Secretary General of the Central Tibet Working Coordination Small Group. He also accompanied CPPCC Chairman Yu Zhengsheng during his trip to Tibetan areas in Sichuan in February 2013. He has been quoted in China's official media as recently on June 2017.

Ye Xiaowen: Ye Xiaowen is an orthodox Communist ideologue and former head of the State Administration for Religious Affairs (SARA) under the State Council. He served in Guizhou Province when Hu Jintao was Party Secretary and his rise coincided with that of Hu Jintao. It was during his tenure at SARA that all controversial legislation about State approval of reincarnate lamas in Tibetan Buddhism was passed. In 2012, Ye Xiaowen was appointed Party Secretary and Vice President of the Institute of Socialism in the rank of Vice Minister in the UFWD. Unlike his predecessors at the Institute, Ye Xiaowen has used this platform to publish a number of articles on Party ideology. He is a member of the 18th Party Central Committee. He will continue to be a factor when the subject of religion in Tibet comes up.

Ye Xiaowen was selected for national politics when he wrote an article based on his time in the Communist Youth League (CYL) describing why many Chinese youth were choosing religion and advocating a more moderate religious policy. In 1995, he became the Director of the Bureau of Religious Affairs under the State Council and worked to prevent religious unrest, select the 11th Panchen Lama and ban the Falungong. He continued as Director after the Bureau of Religious Affairs was renamed in 1998 as the State Administration for Religious Affairs (SARA). Ye Xiaowen was appointed to direct the Central Institute of Socialism in 2009.

Wang Zuo'an: Wang Zuo'an replaced Ye Xiaowen as Director of SARA and is an Alternate Member of the 18th CCP CC. By virtue of his position he will play a role in religious affairs pertaining to Tibet.

Meng Jianzhu: As a member of the Politburo and Minister of Public Security, Meng Jianzhu sits atop one of the key policy input bureaucracies influencing Tibet policy. He is also a member of the powerful Central Political and Legal Committee and the Central Social Management Comprehensive Administration Committee.

Yang Huanning: A former Vice Minister of Public Security (MPS), Yang Huanning is presently a member of the 18th CCP CC. He is China's foremost expert on counter-terrorism and much of his time is spent on issues directly relating to Tibet and Xinjiang. He sits on virtually all the Central level committees and commissions dealing with the security of Tibet. He will definitely provide important inputs on all Tibet-related policies.

Ma Kai: Ma Kai is a member of the Politburo and Vice Premier. He has had a close and enduring relationship with Tibet beginning in the early to mid 1990s under former Premier Zhu Rongji's leadership. As Secretary General of the State Council for a decade, Ma Kai regularly liaised with the TAR leadership and this interaction increased under Wen Jiabao when Ma Kai became Director of the State Development and Reform Commission as well as Director of the State Council Leading Small Group on the Development of the West Region; and member of the Central Committee Tibet Work Coordination Small Group. The latter two organizations have been particularly important in formulating the development strategies of Tibet. Ma Kai will remain important in the formulation of the Tibet policy.

Others of Influence on Tibet issues

Lt General Niu Zhizhong: Lt General Niu Zhizhong was in the TAR between 2000 and the end of 2003 and today is Chief of Staff of the PAP. He visited Colombo in May 2014. He is an Alternate Member of the 18th CCP CC.

Kang Jinzhong: Kang Jinzhong was in the TAR from 2006 through mid 2009 and is now Political Commissar of the National PAP Forestry Headquarters.

Major General Wang Xianghua: Wang Xianghua is Political Commissar of the PAP in the TAR. The PAP and the Ministry of Public Security Ministry, which has operational control of the PAP Border Defense troops in Tibet, carry considerable authority when it comes to the Tibet policy.

Lt. General Wang Zengben: He was Political Commissar of the Tibet Military District and a member of the TAR Standing Committee between 2007 and 2010, but was transferred midway through 2010 and appointed Political Commissar of the Hong Kong PLA Garrison Command. Coinciding with Tian Xiusi's elevation to General, Wang Zengben was transferred back to southwest China as Deputy Political Commissar of the Chengdu Military Region. He is now likely to be one of the influential Tibet experts at the Military Region level in Chengdu. Lt General Wang Zengben was a particular favorite of

Zhang Qingli and completely shared Zhang Qingli's tough approach to law & order and national security issues.

Lt General Tong Guishan: In 2007, Lt. General Tong Guishan was Commander of the Tibet Military Region and had spent almost his entire career of 40 years exclusively in Tibet. For the PLA, this sort of tenure in one place is very rare. In 2008, Tong Guishan was transferred out of Tibet to become one of the Deputy Commanders of the Chengdu Military Region. He retired in late 2009, but will definitely be tapped for his vast knowledge and expertise on matters relating to Tibet.

Lt. General Lang Youliang: 60-year old Lt. General Lang Youliang is Political Commissar of the Tibet Military District. This is Lang Youliang's second posting in Tibet and he has more on-the-ground Tibet experience than Yang Jinshan.

APPENDIX-II

DELEGATES REPRESENTING TIBET AUTONOMOUS REGION AT 19TH PARTY CONGRESS (OCTOBER-NOVEMBER 2017)

The Tibet Autonomous Region (TAR) selected the following 29 Delegates to represent it at the 19th Party Congress in Beijing in October-November 2017:

Ding Yexian, Ma Shengchang, Wang Yongjun, Ba Zhen (Female Tibetan), Pema Yangchen (Female Menba nationality), Pema Wangdue (Tibetan), Nyima Dangqu (Tibetan), Penpa Tashi (Tibetan Party Committee), Penpa Tashi (Tibetan Xietong County), Da Boer (Lhoba nationality), Zhu Zhongkui, Ren Houmin, Xiang Batashi (Tibetan), Xiangba Pincao (Tibetan), Choedon la (Tibetan), Tsering Paldon (Female Tibetan), Tsering Yangchen (Female Tibetan), Xu Chengcang, Wu Yingjie, Zhang Yangqing (Tibetan), Abu (Chinese), Lhatso (Female Tibetan), Sonji Tashi (Tibetan), Lhopon Dhondup (Tibetan), Lobsang Jangsem (Tibetan), Yao Chi (Female Tibetan), Tan Haiyu (Female), Ceng Wanming, Jampa Dolma (Female Tibetan).

ANNEXURE-I

LIST OF MONASTERIES

TIBETAN BUDDHIST MONASTERIES IN THE INDO-HIMALAYAN REGION

S.No.	Monastery	State	Location	Sector
1.	Sertang	Arunachal Pradesh		
2.	Tawang	Arunachal Pradesh		Gelugpa
3.	Cilim	Arunachal Pradesh		
4.	Nyongma	Arunachal Pradesh		
5.	Sarong	Arunachal Pradesh		
6.	Khingmey/khinmey	Arunachal Pradesh		Nyingma
7.	Singsurba	Arunachal Pradesh		
8.	Gyuto	Arunachal Pradesh		Gelugpa
9.	Lower	Arunachal Pradesh		Gelugpa
10.	Sharo	Arunachal Pradesh		Gelugpa
11.	Brache	Arunachal Pradesh		
12.	Ganden Rabgyal Ling	Arunachal Pradesh		Gelugpa
13.	Zharmang	Arunachal Pradesh		
14.	Kinagze	Arunachal Pradesh		
15.	Tamagon	Arunachal Pradesh		
16.	Tashichelen	Arunachal Pradesh		
17.	Chortten	Arunachal Pradesh		
18.	HRO Brakarpo	Arunachal Pradesh		
19.	Manilhagang	Arunachal Pradesh		
20.	Sanga Choeling	Arunachal Pradesh		Nyingmapa
21.	Lagyari	Arunachal Pradesh		Gelugpa
22.	Jang Chop Choeling	Arunachal Pradesh		Gelugpa
23.	Payul Jang Chup Oarge Ling Liung	Arunachal Pradesh		Nyingmapa
24.	Khastong	Arunachal Pradesh		Gelugpa
25.	Thimbang	Arunachal Pradesh		Gelugpa
26.	Gonpa-Tse	Arunachal Pradesh		Gelugpa
27.	Gyangong	Arunachal Pradesh		
28.	Sangthopari	Arunachal Pradesh		
29.	Bramidung-Chune	Arunachal Pradesh		

S.No.	Monastery	State	Location	Sector
30.	Taksang	Arunachal Pradesh		
31.	Samrum	Arunachal Pradesh		
32.	Phalung	Arunachal Pradesh		
33.	Rigya	Arunachal Pradesh		Gelugpa
34.	Tsangpo Rong	Arunachal Pradesh		Gelugpa
35.	Orama Oongchung		Gelugpa	
36.	Khinmey		Nyingmapa	
37.	Khingsar			
38.	Tashi Choeling			
39.	Oevakota			
40.	Kahao	Oibrugarh		
41.	Yortong	Oibrugarh		
42.	Tuting	Oibrugarh		
43.	Oevakota	Oibrugarh		
44.	Gelling	Gelling (Oibrugarh) -		
45.	Choephiling	Miao (Oibrugarh)		
46.	Singha	Singha (Oibrugarh		
47.	Tashi Gong	Tashi Gang (Oibrugarh)		
48.	Ugyen Choeling	Tezu (Oibrugarh)		
49.	Jangchup Choeling	Tezu (Oibrugarh)		
50.	Tashi Choeling	Tezu (Dibrugarh)		
51.	Tuting	Tuting (Dibrugarh)		
52.	Thuptan Osel	Chango		
	Rabgyeling			
53.	Khargog	Chango		
54.	Lakhang	Chango		
55.	Thum	Chango		
56.	Pema Rigzin Ling	Dharamsala	Nyingmapa	
57.	Zilnon	Dharamsala	Nyingmapa	
58.	Rigzin Namdroling	Dharamsala	Nyingmapa	
59.	Key	Kaza, Lahul Spiti		
60.	Tirasang	Kinnaur		
61.	Ribba	Kinnaur	Gelugpa	

S.No.	Monastery	State	Location	Sector
62.	Skiba	Kinnaur	Gelugpa	
63.	Rispa	Kinnaur	Gelugpa	
64.	Akpa	Kinnaur	Drukpa	
65.	Labrang	Kinnaur		
66.	Nako	Kinnaur		
67.	Tabo	Lahul Spiti		
68.	New Gungri	Lahul Spiti		
69.	Gungri	Lahul Spiti		
70.	Morang	Morang	Drukpa	
71.	Charang	Morang	Drukpa	
72.	Khadra	Morang	Drukpa	
73.	Sherap Choeling Nunnery	Morang		
74.	Rarang	Morang	Drukpa	
75.	Jangi	Morang	Drukpa	
76.	Thangi	Morang	Gelugpa	
77.	Spillow	Morang	Drukpa	
78.	Yangchen Choeling	Pangmo, Spiti		
79.	Chuling	Pooh, Kinnaur		
80.	Kanak	Pooh, Kinnaur		
81.	Roppa	Pooh, Kinnaur		
82.	Sunam	Pooh, Kinnaur		
83.	Spillon	Pooh, Kinnaur		
84.	Rustlang	Pooh, Kinnaur		
85.	Khab	Pooh, Kinnaur		
86.	Hango	Pooh, Kinnaur		
87.	Dubling	Pooh, Kinnaur		
88.	Gyabang	Pooh, Kinnaur		
89.	Pooh	Pooh, Kinnaur		
90.	Namgia	Pooh, Kinnaur		
91.	Nesang	Pooh, Kinnaur		
92.	Saiso	Pooh, Kinnaur		
93.	Tangyud	Shimla		
94.	Shey	Ladakh		
95.	Phugtal	Ladakh		
96.	Alchi	Ladakh		

S.No.	Monastery	State	Location	Sector
97.	Zongkhul	Ladakh		
9S.	Namgyal Tsemo	Ladakh		
99.	Rangdum	Ladakh		
100.	Saini	Ladakh		
101.	Stongdey	Ladakh		
102.	Hemis	Ladakh	Drukpa Kargyu	
103.	Cave	Ladakh		
104.	Shachikul	Ladakh	Dregong Kargyu	
105.	Kargyu	Ladakh	Karma Kargyu	
106.	Chimey	Ladakh	Karma Kargyu	
107.	Stakna	Ladakh	Drukpa Kargyu	
108.	Sokti Rimpoche	Ladakh	Nunnery	
109.	Takthok	Ladakh	Nyingma	
110.	Tashe Choling	Ladakh	Nyingma	
111.	Thiksey	Ladakh	Gelugpa	
112.	Matho	Ladakh	Sakya	
113.	Skurbachan	Ladakh	Dregong Kargyu	
114.	Phayang	Ladakh	Dregong Kargyu	
115.	Lamayuru	Ladakh	Dregong Kargyu	
116.	Nyoma	Ladakh	Drukpa Kargyu	
117.	Spituk	Ladakh	Gelugpa	
118.	Likir	Ladakh	Gelugpa	
119.	Chumar	Ladakh	Nyingma	
120.	Deskit	Ladakh	Selugpa	
121.	Hanie	Ladakh	Drukpa Kargyu	
122.	Sanker	Ladakh	Selugpa	

S.No.	Monastery	State	Location	Sector
123.	Stok	Ladakh	Selugpa	
124.	Sabu	Ladakh	Selugpa	
125.	Samstaniing	Ladakh	Selugpa	
126.	Chemrey	Ladakh	Drukpa Kargyu	
127.	Mahe	Ladakh	Karma Kargyu	
128.	Rudok	Ladakh	Karma Kargyu	
129.	Rizong	Ladakh	Geiugpa Kargyu	
130.	Fudong		Karma Kargyu	
131.	Rumtek		Karma Kargyu	
132.	Pemayangtse		Karma Kargyu	
133.	Guru Kubum			
	Lhakhang			
134.	Kagoan	Chandmari		
	Tshechoeiingi			
135.	Rankha	East Sikkim		
136.	Guru Lhakhang	Gangtok	Nyingmapa	
137.	Ngor	Gangtok	Sakya	
138.	Chorten/Deoraii	Gangtok	Nyingmapa	
139.	Rangkha	Gangtok	Karma Kargyu	
140.	Gongang	Gangtok	Nyingmapa	
	Chokariing			
141.	Dodrup Chen Çhorten	Gangtok	Nyingmapa	
142.	Geiup	Gnathang	Geiugpa	
143.	Sa-Ngor Chostshog centre	Gongnye		
144.	Lachen	Lachen	Nyingmapa	
145.	Paichen Choeiing	Raiang	Karma Kargyu	

S.No.	Monastery	State	Location	Sector
146.	Raiang/Paichen Choeiing	South Sikkim	Karma Kargyu	
147.	Taktse Institute	Taktse		
148.	Thupten Chhokhorling	Thangu		
149.	Bungoan Zamon Gen	Dehradun		
150.	Saqoan Sechan Tenpay Gasel	Dehradun		
151.	Sakya Tangoan Rinchen Choeling	Dehradun		
152.	Sanor Abun Choeling	Dehradun		
153.	Sagoan Dongkar Chothey	Dehradun		
154.	Gyagoan Tashi Keyal	Dehradun		
155.	Kagoan Deychen Chokarling	Dehradun		
156.	Niggoan Tiktsi Tsichen	Dehradun		
157.	Kagoan Degoan Jangchup	Dehradun		
158.	Gyagoan Sadup Chopal	Mussoorie		
159.	Sakya College	Dehradun		
160.	Gyagoan Lodak Donneykaling	Dehradun		
161.	Niggoan Gaselling	Dehradun		
162.	Photang	Kalimpong		
163.	ZakharChoedhe	Kalimpong		
	Singker Cheodo			
164.	Kargyu Thak	Kalimpong		
	Choeling			
165.	Gayden Choeling	Darjeeling (Sukhia Nyingmapa Pokhari)		
166.	Zigar Chostruh	Darjeeling		
	Shedupling			
167.	Shamtencholling	Darjeeling		
168.	Druk Sangnag Choeling	Darjeeling		
169.	Tsechu Lhakhang	Darjeeling		
170.	Gyanjan Samten Chopen	Darjeeling		

S.No.	Monastery	State	Location	Sector
171.	Boka Nagthong Choeling	Darjeeling		
172.	Phuntsok Pema Choeling	Darjeeling		
173.	Guru Sakya	Darjeeling		
174.	Phuntsok Nayap Choeling	Darjeeling		
175.	Ganden Tashi Choeling	Darjeeling		
176.	Yiga Choeling	Darjeeling		
177.	Pema Choeling	Darjeeling	Nyingmapa	
178.	Samtan Choeling	Darjeeling	Gelugpa	
179.	Kalu Rimpoche	Darjeeling	Karma Kargyu	
180.	Thupsten Sanga Choeling	Darjeeling	Drukpa Kargyu	
181.	Ogyan Kunsang Chokorling	Darjeeling		
182.	Sand rub Darjay Choeiling	Darjeeling		
183.	Sed Gyued	Kalimpong	Gelugpa	
184.	Sangchen Dorjee	Kalimpong		
185.	Deewakar Vihara	Kalimpong	Karma Kargyu	
186.	Kagyue	Kalimpong	Nyingmapa	
187.	Jangsa Dechen Choeling	Kalimpong	Nyingmapa	
188.	Drongsar	Kalimpong	Nyingmapa	
189.	Gaden Thapa Choeling	Kalimpong	Gelugpa	
190.	Rhey Gyuepa	Kalimpong	Gelugpa	
191.	Zandhok Palri	Kalimpong	Nyingmapa	
192.	Sangtok Phari	Kalimpong	Nyingmapa	

ANNEXURE-II

TALKS BETWEEN THE ENVOYS OF THE DALAI LAMA AND THE CHINESE OFFICIALS

April 24, 1982 – A high level Tibetan delegation arrives in Beijing to hold exploratory talks with Chinese officials. The delegation, composed of P.T. Taklha, Juchen Thubten Namgyal and Lodi Gyari, made no substantive headway.

October 19, 1984 – The three-member exploratory delegation holds a second round of talks with Chinese leaders. Again, no progress toward substantive negotiations is made.

September 9-24, 2002 – Following a nine-year impasse, contact between Beijing and the Tibetan-government-in-exile resumed when the Dalai Lama's Special Envoy, Lodi Gyari, led a delegation of four to Beijing and Lhasa. The trip was intended to create an atmosphere conducive for substantive negotiations. The team included Kelsang Gyaltsen, Envoy of the Dalai Lama and two senior assistants, Sonam N. Dagpo and Bhuchung K. Tsering.

May 25-June 8, 2003 – A second round of talks is held between envoys of the Dalai Lama and the Chinese leadership during the Tibetan team's trip to Beijing and parts of Tibet. The Tibetans characterize the nature of these trips as "confidence building measures."

September 12-29, 2004 – A third round of talks is held between envoys of the Dalai Lama and the Chinese leadership during the Tibetan team's trip to Beijing and parts of Tibet. The international community viewed these visits as positive steps forward, but few governments made legitimate efforts to bring both parties to the negotiation table.

May 23, 2004 – The Chinese government issued a 30-page White Paper on Tibet aimed at dampening expectations by Tibetans for genuine autonomy. The White Paper was seen as a negotiating tactic to underscore the resistance of hardliners to move forward in good faith.

June 30, July 1, 2005 – A fourth round of meetings between the Tibetan team and the Chinese leadership is held in Bern, Switzerland. The Tibetans say that the trip is designed to "move the ongoing process to a new level of engagement aimed at bringing about substantive negotiations to achieve a mutually acceptable solution to the Tibetan issue". Meanwhile, China continues to publicly criticize the Dalai Lama and reiterates its long-standing preconditions to negotiations.

February 15-23, 2006 – The Dalai Lama's envoys met in Guilin, China. In previous meetings, the envoys had requested to visit other autonomous regions of China, which is why Guangxi Autonomous Region was chosen. After the meetings concluded, Lodi Gyari reported that there was "a growing understanding between the two sides, though fundamental differences persisted." However, he made clear that the Tibetans remain committed to the dialogue process and are hopeful that progress will be possible by continuing the engagement.

A full transcript of Lodi Gyari's briefing, "The Current State of Discussions between the Dalai Lama and the Government of the People's Republic of China" (A John L. Thornton China Center and Center for Northeast Asian Policy Studies Briefing) is available at the website of the Brookings Institution at http://www.brook.edu/fp/china/events/20061114.pdf.

June 29 to July 5, 2007 – The Dalai Lama's envoys were hosted by the UFWD in Shanghai and Nanjing. Following this meeting the envoys reported that "our dialogue process has reached a critical stage" and that "we…made some concrete proposals for implementation if our dialogue process is to go forward."

May 8, 2008 – The Dalai Lama's envoys reported back on talks with officials from the United Front Work Department in Shenzhen, China, on Sunday [May 4]. Special Envoy Lodi Gyari, speaking to the press in Dharamsala, India, after briefing the Dalai Lama, referred to the significance of a comment by Chinese President and Party Secretary Hu Jintao on May 3, 2008 that "our attitude towards contacts and consultation with the Dalai Lama is serious". Lodi Gyari said: "It is welcome that the leader of such an important nation stands in front of the world and says that China is serious about the relationship at the highest level. Not only was it a direct comment about the recent meeting that took place, but it was also in the context of a historic press conference [with Japanese PM Yasuo Fukuda]." President Hu's visit to Tokyo marks the first time in 10 years that a Chinese President has visited Japan, and is widely regarded as an effort to repair strained relations between the two nations. Lodi Gyari added that it was encouraging because many Tibetans as well as many world leaders were skeptical, for good reason, about the dialogue process.

October 31, 2008 – The Tibetan Envoys presented the Chinese side with a Memorandum on Genuine Autonomy for the Tibetan People when they visited China for the eighth round of talks. Special Envoy Lodi Gyari and Envoy Kelsang Gyaltsen, accompanied by senior aides Sonam N. Dagpo and Bhuchung K. Tsering, both members of the Task Force on Negotiations, and Kalsang Tsering from the Secretariat of the Task Force, visited China from October 30 to November 5, 2008. They returned to India on November 6, 2008.

During the seventh round of talks in Beijing on July 1and 2, 2008, the Vice Chairman of the Chinese People's Political Consultative Conference and the Minister of the Central United Front Work Department, Du Qinglin, explicitly invited suggestions from His Holiness the Dalai Lama for the stability and development of Tibet. The Executive Vice Minister of the Central United Front Work Department, Zhu Weiqun, further said they would like to hear Tibetan views on the degree or form of autonomy they were seeking as well as on all aspects of regional autonomy within the scope of the Constitution of the People's Republic of China.

November 2008 – The first Special General Meeting of Tibetans was held in Dharamsala from November 17 to 22, 2008. Over 581 delegates from 19 countries participated.

The meeting reaffirmed the Tibetan commitment to follow the Middle Way Approach. The meeting called upon the Tibetan leadership to terminate the ongoing talks with the Chinese leadership if the Chinese Government does not reciprocate positively to the overtures of the Tibetan people.

January 26 to 31, 2010 – Special Envoy Lodi Gyari and Envoy Kelsang Gyaltsen, accompanied by two members of Task Force on Negotiations, Tenzin P. Atisha and Bhuchung K. Tsering, and Jigmey Passang from the Task Force Secretariat, visited China from January 26 to 31, 2010, for the ninth round of discussions with representatives of the Chinese leadership. This was after a gap of nearly 14 months.

On January 26, 2010, they formally presented to the Chinese side a Note relating to the Memorandum on Genuine Autonomy for the Tibetan People that had been given during the previous eighth round in November 2008. The Note contained seven points that addressed the fundamental issues raised by the Chinese leadership during the eighth round and some constructive suggestions for a way forward in the dialogue process. The Chinese Government has made different comments and expression of concerns regarding the Memorandum and the Note was intended to address these and to offer some constructive suggestions for a way forward in the dialogue process. The Note was also intended to prevent the chance of misinterpretation and misconception by the general public.
They met Du Qinglin, Vice Chairman of the Chinese People's Political Consultative Conference as well as Minister of the Central United Front Work Department, on January 30. They had a day-long discussion with Executive Vice Minister Zhu Weiqun and Vice Minister Sithar on January 31, 2010.

Since then there have been no further rounds of discussions between the two sides.

Annexure III

Greater Tibet

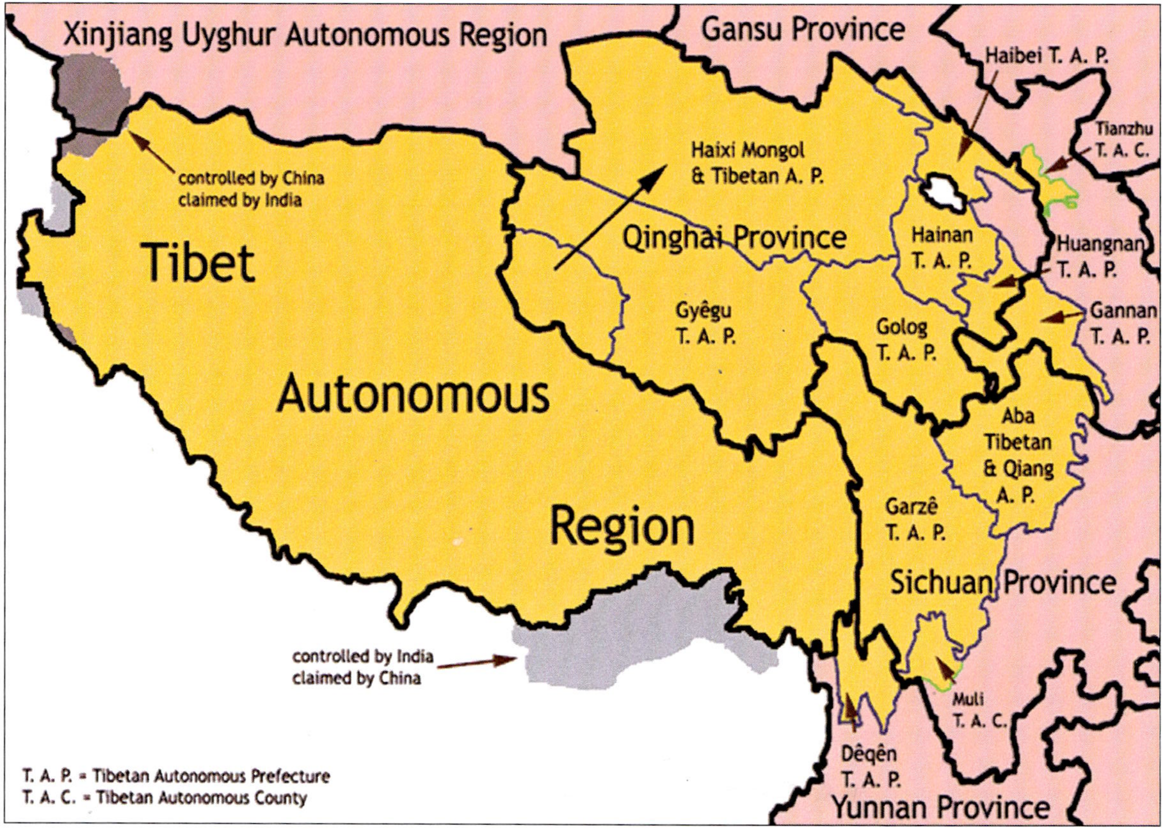

Source: https://www.google.co.in/search?q=map+of+greater+Tibet&tbm=isch&imgil=4x2Mfww-bGwOMM%253A%253BanCFfVd4ZLbdwM%253Bhttps%25253A%25252F%25252Fcommons.wikimedia.org%25252Fwiki%25252FAtlas_of_Tibet&source=iu&pf=m&fir=4x2Mfww-bGwOMM%253A%252CanCFfVd4ZLbdwM%252C_&usg=__nRJulg55ie0tW6isa1KuQjtjOHg%3D&biw=1584&bih=753&ved=0ahUKEwihvLzSxoPWAhUGLI8KHRp5CuoQyjcIMg&ei=_RepWeHJG4bYvASa8qnQDg#imgrc=4x2Mfww-bGwOMM:

INDEX